"*Think to Win* demonstrates that winning is not just about planning. The best-laid plans are worthless unless they're communicated broadly, understood widely, and viewed with a sense of urgency to act. This book gives us the essentials for bringing everything together—from thinking to planning to acting to winning."

Brian Kelley, President and CEO, Keurig Green Mountain

"*Think to Win* shows business leaders how to extend strategic thinking out of the purview of the 'elite few' and into the company culture as a whole. It's a simple, proven approach to analyzing and solving old or new challenges and provides a common language anyone at any level in the organization can understand."

Joseph E. Scalzo, President and Chief Executive Officer,
Atkins Nutritionals, Inc.

"For those leaders who have struggled to improve strategic thinking throughout their organizations, *Think to Win* provides a tried and tested approach that works with companies large and small. And since the best-thought-out plans in the world are worthless unless you make them happen, *Think to Win* has a roadmap for executing with excellence."

Richard H. Lenny, former Chairman and CEO,
The Hershey Company

"*Think to Win* shows the benefits of thinking both strategically and simply. The ability to think-plan-act with clarity makes a difference. Organizations perform better over time with leaders and managers who can spot and avoid things that are distractions and time-wasters and focus on the few things that produce sustained results."

John A. Quelch, Harvard Business School, Charles Edward
Wilson Professor of Business Administration

"If you want to help your organization grow, *Think to Win* is a must-read book. With the constantly changing demands of all business, day-to-day challenges dominate our lives. But strategic thinking has never been more important. And *Think to Win* shows how strategic thinking can become part of the fabric of every organization and every person in it."

Kelly J. Haecker, The WhiteWave Foods Company, Chief Financial Officer and Executive Vice President

"*Think to Win* is more than a fool-proof approach for making strategic thinking accessible to everyone. It's a way of looking at all aspects of business with an open mind that challenges all assumptions, engages the entire organization, and drives superior performance."

Jim Holbrook, President and CEO, Post Consumer Brands

"*Think to Win* shows business leaders the importance of ensuring strategic thinking is not viewed as the purview of the "elite few" and is embedded in the company culture as a whole. It's a simple, proven approach to analyzing and solving old or new challenges and provides a common language anyone at any level in the organization can understand. This is the key to turning strategy into execution and delivering superior marketplace results."

Sandra (Sandi) E. Peterson, Johnson & Johnson Group Worldwide Chairman and member of the Executive Committee.

"Paul, John, and Peter have hit a home run with *Think to Win*. Strategy is not about budgeting, and it's not executing to incremental goals. It's thinking differently about what can be done and how to make that happen. What's needed is different thinking combined with a shared language and tools to make it happen. They've pulled it off. *Think to Win* is about how to differentiate your business in the eyes of target customers and create the conditions where they would rather work with you than with anyone else. This is so much easier said than done. The good news is the authors have been implementing these ideas for many years and have a track record of success."

Norm Smallwood, coauthor of Results-Based Leadership *and* The Leadership Code

"The five principles of *Think to Win* are a game changer in strategic thinking. The brilliance is in the simplicity of the process, which begins by ensuring you ask the right questions so you identify the right area to focus upon. This book is practical, filled with case examples and how-tos. The process works for organizations and for individuals. Utilizing these five principles is definitely a formula for winning!"

Dana Robinson, coauthor of Performance Consulting *and* Strategic Business Partner

"*Think to Win* is powerful and insightful. Applying the principles of *Think to Win* allows leaders to move their businesses forward by knowing what's most important for their consumers and customers and then acting."

Rob De Martini, President and Chief Executive Officer, New Balance Inc.

"*Think to Win* is an important and timely book. The principles and practices outlined by the authors, when applied to any organization, will not only build capability in leaders to quickly identify and address business challenges, they also serve to unify organizations around a common language. All are essential to win in the marketplace."

Edward F. Lonergan, former Chief Executive Officer of Chiquita Brands International, Inc. and Diversy, Inc.

"*Think to Win* is that one book that every executive must read and must have their teams read. Their model for strategic thinking is a proven approach to help teams face complex business challenges and achieve extraordinary results. Their approach can be easily implemented and woven into the fabric of an organization so that this becomes the way you think and work."

Andrea G. Procaccino, CMT, Vice President and Chief Learning Officer, New York Presbyterian Hospital

"Smart and simple. Those two words describe the *Think to Win* philosophy and approach. In our hyper-accelerated world, we need a durable yet flexible approach to making the right things happen to grow and sustain our business. *Think to Win* gets after the right balance of discipline, focus, alignment, and flexibility. Finally, a model that focuses on outcomes, not just activity."

Joe Garbus, Vice President of Talent and Leadership,
Celgene Corporation

"*Think to Win* is a wonderful resource for leaders who want to create an atmosphere where there is an openness and willingness to share knowledge and develop effective strategies that deliver great results."

Dr. Leon Bruner, Senior Vice President for Scientific and
Regulatory Affairs and Chief Science Officer,
Grocery Manufacturers Association.

THINK
TO
WIN

UNLEASHING THE POWER OF
STRATEGIC THINKING

PAUL BUTLER
JOHN MANFREDI
PETER KLEIN

New York   Chicago   San Francisco   Athens   London
Madrid   Mexico City   Milan   New Delhi
Singapore   Sydney   Toronto

1234567890   DOC/DOC   121098765

ISBN: 978-0-07-184095-8
MHID: 0-07-184095-8

e-ISBN: 978-0-07-184096-5
e-MHID: 0-07-184096-6

McGraw-Hill Education books are available at special quantity discounts to use as
premiums and sales promotions, or for use in corporate training programs. To contact
a representative, please visit the Contact Us page at www.mhprofessional.com.

CONTENTS

ACKNOWLEDGMENTS   v

INTRODUCTION: 1

CHAPTER 1: New Thinking for Winning   5

CHAPTER 2: Principles for Winning   15

CHAPTER 3: What It Takes to Win   39

CHAPTER 4: Key To Winning   67

CHAPTER 5: Vision: Seeing the Future of Winning   83

CHAPTER 6: Strategies: Making the Right Choices   101

CHAPTER 7: Confronting the Elusive:
Moving from Planning to Acting   117

CHAPTER 8: Bringing Everything Together:
From Thinking to Acting to Winning   139

CHAPTER 9: The Winning Never Ends: Anchoring Change   163

EPILOGUE: Turning Over the Hourglass   183

APPENDIX A: Organizational Alignment Survey   189

APPENDIX B: Think to Win Situation Assessment Diagnostic:
Situation Assessment Tool for Consumer/
Customer Marketing   197

GLOSSARY   211

INDEX   215

ACKNOWLEDGMENTS

In many ways, our book owes its existence to the hundreds of alumni of *Think to Win* workshops and programs, who over the years asked us to capture the principles and process of TTW in a form that would serve as a refresher for them and as an introduction for their uninitiated associates. Their enthusiasm for the results achieved, as well as our own deep-seated belief in the transformative value of TTW, led us take on what has been a challenging, time-consuming, but also very rewarding effort.

With us each step of the way were Mary Glenn, associate publisher at McGraw Hill Professional, and Margret McBride, our one-of-a-kind literary agent. Their commitment to our book and its potential impact were essential to it seeing the light of day. Margret also helped shape our preliminary thoughts into a cogent proposal. Her associate, Faye Atcheson, also provided valuable assistance and feedback, especially at critical times.

Special acknowledgement and thanks go to each of the people we interviewed in preparing our book. The insights, observations and stories of some of these associates are an important part of our book. While many others—including Eric Amour, Mark Bertolami, Roger Deromedi, Joe Dooley, Stephanie Franklin, Ned Guillet, Blair Hawley, Carole Herman, Bryan Hesse, Rick Kash, Ed Lonergan, Nancy Reardon, Alan Sequeira, and Ken Sobaski—are not directly referenced, they were no less important. Their words and thoughts greatly informed our thinking as we wrote the book.

Contributing to the drafting were Digby and Kay Diehl, whose distinguished careers include writing numerous books, reporting and editing for newspapers, radio, and television, film and movie criticism, and serving as university lecturers. Their efforts are greatly appreciated.

John acknowledges the lessons learned from his many associates during his career with several consumer product companies and as head of a consulting company and as writer and business book author. He especially acknowledges the leadership and mentorship of James M. Kilts, CEO of both Nabisco Foods and Gillette, where John served on the senior management teams. Jim, who championed the TTW approach throughout his career, broadened John's understanding of how to win in business by doing what matters—for the business and all its stakeholders, especially the associates, by encouraging them to learn, develop, and grow, and rewarding them for their performance.

Also important to John are the senior leaders of the client companies he has counseled over the years, people with special capabilities, who invariably distinguished themselves and their companies—leaders like James White of Jamba Juice, who demonstrated the importance of vision, commitment, and integrity to achieving transformational change and success.

John would also like to thank his loving family, his wife Doreen, and daughters Hadley, Kendre, and Nicole and her family for their support and encouragement. Doreen worked tirelessly editing and proofing each chapter, providing constructive criticism throughout. Her efforts made a big difference in many aspects of our book.

Paul first acknowledges and dedicates this book to his wife Becky, whose ongoing love, support, and belief in him, has made a difference in his life. Because of her, he feels like the true winner! He would also like to thank his children Jim, Erin, and Lindsay, who are constant reminders to him of what is most important!

He would also like to thank his partners and associates at GlobalEdg—especially Sally Arconti, Bonnie Bauer, Jack Mastrianni, Emma Huebenthal, June McPherson, and Brian Somma, whose review and contributions to the manuscript were extremely helpful.

There are other behind the scenes individuals whose contributions need to be recognized: Dana Robinson, Diane Ramos, Mark Safferstone, Kerry Robinson, and Norm Smallwood's inspiration, insights, and friendship.

In addition to his Gillette colleagues, Paul truly appreciates his many clients who help him to grow, learn, and sharpen his techniques and tools. It is an honor and a privilege to collaborate with so many of them.

Peter acknowledges the importance of his career of 45+ years working at and with over 40 consumer product companies and three consultancies—Marketing Corporation of America, The Cambridge Group, and his own PK Associates—in addition, he has witnessed the TTW model and process succeed in delivering results at Kraft Foods, Nabisco Foods, Gillette, and other companies. He thanks the many people throughout his career on both sides of the desk from whom he learned. He borrowed a few key takeaways from many of them for which he is deeply appreciative and apologetic if any show up in the book not appropriately credited. Peter also thanks the folks who provided testimonials for our book. Critically important, he thanks his wife Anne and his children Alex and Liz and their families (Sandy, Gary, Misha, Xander, Zachary, and Dylan) for their constant love, support, and ability to make him laugh.

Introduction

Is there a simple approach to decision making and strategic thinking that can really work? Winning, especially in today's environment of global hypercompetitiveness, must require complex algorithms and abstruse conceptual paradigms that go well beyond easy comprehension. Something that can be easily understood, quickly applied, and not only identify great strategic options, but also great approaches to execute them, really can't exist. Or can it?

Yes, it can. And we've written *Think to Win* to show how it does.

There is nothing wrong with the hundreds of other approaches presented in books, business review articles and academic research treatises that promise great strategic thinking results. But they do have limitations. Most are intended for the select few who have backgrounds enabling them to comprehend, integrate, and apply these advanced concepts and approaches. Others are more broadly accessible but require extended rigorous training to allow the approaches to be applied. And still others work in certain categories or sectors, or on certain issues and problems, but not widely, and almost never across the board.

And this is where and why *Think to Win* is different. Its easy accessibility; its understandability at a near universal level; and its usefulness across an entire range of business, professional, and personal issues are exceptional. We know of nothing that even begins to approach it.

So we've written *Think to Win* (*TTW*) to disclose the power of this approach by providing the principles and processes that propel *TTW*, along with many illustrative case histories and examples, based on our decades of experience as senior leaders of several top global companies and as consultants to scores of others. In this book, you'll find first-person accounts, composite case studies, and guidance from experts.

We provide a simple, proven approach for analyzing issues, challenges, and any difficult problems whether they've been around a long time, or suddenly hit you broadside. Our approach strips away all the complexity.

We offer a system and language that work at an individual level and also throughout the organization. It's a unifying process and language—a common approach from the top of the organization to the bottom, no matter where anyone is located across the country, or around the globe.

Think to Win eliminates assumptions, guesswork, and misunderstandings from the get-go. Things get moving immediately, and the tools and frameworks we offer in this book facilitate the flow. The net effect goes well beyond producing one-time wins. It becomes part of the new culture that defines the on-going success of any organization. Success becomes something people can begin to count on and invest in—financially and personally. Attitudes change when it becomes common knowledge that the organization is both an exciting and a fulfilling place to be. People bring their best selves to work and the organization thrives.

This is a timely and important book. The ability to think-plan-act makes a difference. Research supports it and our experience confirms it. Organizations that perform better over time have leaders and managers who know how to differentiate between those things that are distractions and wasters of time and energy and those that produce sustained results. That *ability to differentiate* is strategic thinking at its best.

There are real standouts among companies—the winners, the think-to-win powerhouses—that have become game changers in their sectors. This book shares what we have learned from some of the best thinkers in business. And it reveals the inner workings of several of their companies.

We think all of it will give you incredible insights on how to win. And that's what *Think to Win* is all about.

CHAPTER 1

New Thinking for Winning

What if we could show you a new way of thinking—a fast, sure-fire way of assessing, questioning, and determining what is important? A new way of thinking about problems and taking advantage of opportunities? A new way of quickly communicating what's going on, what you're going to do, and what impact your actions would have?

That would be *Think to Win*, a dynamic new approach to thinking simply, yet strategically. That's *TTW, Think to Win*.

This book will help you think to win by giving you the same tools that the winning CEOs and senior managers use every day. They're not likely to share them with you, but our step-by-step approach will. And TTW is so easy that strategic thinking becomes a habitual part of your life. It will help you do a better, smarter job for your company, and it can also lay out your game plan for moving up the ladder, or even reinventing yourself and finding a better position in an entirely new field.

Thinking simply and strategically matters! For the past 20 years, we have applied TTW in hundreds of situations. We've done it with our own companies, and with companies we've worked for. It has solved problems both large and small and maximized literally thousands of opportunities. Whether the organization is a Fortune 500 company, an educational or medical institution, a governmental agency, a small business start-up, a philanthropy or other nonprofit, a family wrestling with major decisions like college or retirement planning, or *you*, plotting out a career trajectory, TTW will point you toward the best outcomes. And it will do it quickly, as well.

We explode one persistent myth about the strategic thinking process: that it is long and cumbersome. Even if that were true in the past, it's not now. TTW is not protracted thinking, the kind that eventually coughs up a 500-page doorstop-type plan that is shelved upon completion. We empower people to create plans that are living documents, guiding decision making on a daily basis. Strategic thinking as we practice it—Think to Win, TTW—is real, actionable and accessible. We're talking about *think-plan-act*—the kind of thinking that quickly galvanizes individuals, companies, and other organizations to produce positive results.

Many companies have generated remarkable successes by creating traditions of strategic thinking. By instilling this capability throughout the organizations, companies such as Keurig, Jamba Juice, Procter & Gamble, Gillette, and New Balance have enjoyed years of dynamic growth. We have included a discussion of just a few here, but in each chapter you will find additional stories of think-to-win successes.

Trusted Everywhere

The rejuvenation of the Duracell Company demonstrates the power of TTW to totally transform a company's culture as well as its performance. When Mark Leckie was named president of Duracell, he faced a formidable challenge. The famed battery maker was in real trouble. Market share had been plummeting for 11 straight quarters and earnings were sinking. When it was acquired by Gillette, Duracell was expected to be one of its elite brands. Instead, it turned into a disaster. As it faltered, it started dragging down Gillette's performance with it, becoming, in the words of a leading business magazine, "the central culprit in Gillette's fall from grace" (from "Can Gillette Regain Its Voltage?" *BusinessWeek*, October 15, 2000).

What was wrong? The Duracell management team was not the problem. Most team members were long-tenured pros, people attuned to all the ins and outs of battery demand. They knew, for example, that during the holidays, prominent placement of battery displays in the toy department gave sales a big boost. And that two days before a hurricane hit, consumers would rush to hardware stores and home improvement centers to stock up on emergency supplies, especially extra batteries. To spur impulse buying year round, they displayed batteries in multiple locations storewide.

There was no question that the Duracell team was dedicated. Team members' work ethics were strong, anything but impediments to performance. Their plans were well-drawn and detailed. Their implementation approaches were well aligned with their plans, and their field resources were marshaled around the right tasks. Leckie had a lot of confidence in them.

Product quality also was not the problem. To the contrary, in an effort to one-up competitors, Duracell had introduced the Ultra, a premium battery with greater longevity, and a premium price to go with it. Designed for the newest generation of power-hungry electronic devices, the battery was supposed to lure tech-savvy customers away from its rivals. The managers who conceived Ultra had migrated to Duracell from Gillette, where trading up consumers was a long-standing strategy for Gillette blades and razors. But instead of grabbing market share from competitors, Ultra sales had come from Coppertop, Duracell's mainstream brand. Even worse, as Ultra and Coppertop were battling for share at retail, rival brands and private label batteries swooped in to undercut them at the lower end of the price spectrum.

To get to the core issues, Mark Leckie listened intently to the presentations by each of his top-level executives. When these managers compared notes afterward, they noted a baffling pattern. All of them had spent a lot less time briefing their new president than they had expected. They had barely begun when Mark would say, "Got it. Let's move on."

What could he see that they could not? How was he absorbing information so swiftly? Mark Leckie was using the power of TTW. He was rapidly analyzing the input his team had given him and using a series of questions, screens, and filters that enabled him to gain insights quickly. The process allowed him to establish a framework that highlighted connections and patterns, and put them into context. TTW not only gave him the power to isolate the problem, but it also enabled him to identify a solution and to plot a series of actions to be taken.

As is true with many insights, Duracell's core problem was obvious—hiding in plain sight—once it was identified. It was Ultra's premium pricing. From the outset, Duracell had assumed that consumers would be willing to pay more for its high-performance battery. But would they?

Products with a premium price must not just be better, they have to readily be *perceived* as better. It's easy for people to tell that a high-priced Gillette blade shaves a lot closer, more smoothly, and more comfortably than a lower-priced competitor.

Not so with batteries. To consumers, batteries are judged on how long they last. But that's very hard to tell. Consider the AAs in a TV remote. Even bargain batteries will power a remote for about three months—long enough for people to forget when they last replaced them. In a busy household, not many consumers would notice that the Ultras lasted longer. And even fewer were willing to pay 30 percent more.

Mark Leckie realized that his team hadn't fully explored the pricing issue. After Ultra was launched, inertia took over. And implementing the Ultra strategy was leading the company over the cliff.

Once the flawed assumption was identified, Leckie steered his team on a major course correction that had a broad and far-ranging impact on virtually every aspect of how the company operated. Duracell restructured how resources were allocated and revisited how it approached marketing, market research, and technical innovation. As pricing gaps with competitors were narrowed, unnecessary costs were removed throughout the company. Research budgets were trimmed, and the company's efforts were redirected away from breakthrough innovations and toward new incremental ways to become more competitive. Sales repositioned Duracell with vendors to increase its presence on mainstream brand shelves. Since the Duracell brand had maintained its excellent reputation with consumers, marketing was redirected to capitalize on this brand trust.

It worked. Mark Leckie's strategic reimagination jumpstarted a turnaround and put Duracell on a new path to profitability. Correcting course gave him the opportunity not only to reinvigorate the Duracell brand, but also to give his team a valuable analytical tool. All Duracell managers received training in TTW and were encouraged to apply the approach to issues both large and small. Now that the company was moving forward again, Leckie knew that the thinking capability he had harnessed to solve one serious problem would also empower his staff and improve day-to-day decision making.

Vital Child's Play

Keeping an established brand fresh but familiar requires a balance that's a challenge to maintain. Sales of Lego, one of the most iconic toys for baby boomers, started falling as the Internet revolution took hold. Children and grandchildren of boomers deserted the classic building blocks in favor of TV, movies, and online entertainment. Initial efforts to appeal to this new digital generation were not successful. And after repeated failed efforts, bankruptcy loomed.

Using a TTW precept led to the key insight. Lego realized it must focus on *one vital issue*. It had to capture the imagination of millennial kids without abandoning what made Lego so popular with their parents—the ability to use their blocks to *tell a story*. And stories need people—characters—not just buildings. So by licensing figures from *Star Wars*, *SpongeBob SquarePants*, *Teenage Mutant Ninja Turtles*, and other popular shows, Lego not only invited young people to put themselves into the action, but it also opened the door so they could use their favorite characters to make up their own stories. Thinking simply yet strategically helped the company innovate while staying true to its origins. And it set the stage for the explosive growth that has made Lego a global brand.

Taking the Long, Strategic View

Keurig pioneered the single-cup coffeemaker and saw explosive growth as a result. As Michelle Stacy, former Keurig president, and her management team launched their thinking about the future of the company, their key strategic insight was the need to focus on *long-term potential*, not just on short-term profits. It was a choice that paid huge dividends.

Keurig had started slowly, with a small range of coffee strengths and flavors along with a high-end brewer that cost $900. In the beginning, the company marketed exclusively to offices, where the $900 price point was less of a hurdle. Keurig's strategy included a plan to market to residential consumers eventually, but deliberately deferred action. This think-to-win mindset allowed Keurig to gain an in-depth understanding of consumer wants, learning from its experience in commercial venues. It also created consumers who understood the product advantages and wanted it for their homes. The added time allowed Keurig to cost-engineer the brewer and lower the price of its coffeemaker.

The data compilation and insights paid dividends. When Keurig started selling to the home market, the product took off. Over a five-year period, Keurig's sales rocketed and drove Keurig Green Mountain sales from approximately $500 million to $4.5 billion, and in the process transformed the way people brew coffee—both in the office and at home. Keurig machines now sit in more than 18 million kitchens, and cost between $79 and $199 apiece. Single-serving coffee pods are available in Keurig's own Green Mountain brand and also in Folgers, Dunkin' Donuts, Starbucks, Peet's Coffee & Tea, and many other brands.

"Programs that transform take patience," Michelle says. "People who make great leaders of breakthrough innovation programs always ask the *What if* question. Speed to market, probability of quick return, and profitability mindsets have to take backseats to truly delivering a product that delights the consumer in every aspect." Thinking that wins.

Object Lessons—Why Companies and People Fail

In contrast, many companies have inflicted great harm on themselves by failing to think strategically. While some, like Duracell, reinvent themselves and enjoy years of dynamic growth, others keep on digging themselves into deeper and deeper holes.

Doubling Down on Bricks and Mortar

When Blockbuster began, it did movie rentals better than anyone, and the market rewarded it. Families roamed the aisles of Blockbuster stores, selecting titles—and movie night snacks—to take home. But success was short-lived. Blockbuster's brick-and-mortar model showed signs of vulnerability as soon as Netflix rolled out its more convenient direct-to-consumer mail-order service. Blockbuster took note, but failed to respond. As technology advanced and Netflix added an on-demand streaming video capability, Blockbuster again failed to react. Company leadership was certain that consumers still wanted a "real store," where they could see—and touch—their choices. Rather than challenging this assumption with hard facts and data-based analysis, Blockbuster doubled down on bricks-and-mortar, adding more stores, which placed an even greater strain on its faltering model. Bankruptcy soon followed.

The Way the Cupcake Crumbles

Crumbs was a successful specialty baked goods company that caught the crest of the cupcake wave. Unfortunately, it assumed the wave would be endless. The company began as a mom-and-pop bakery in an upscale neighborhood of Manhattan. Its stylishly decorated offerings were so popular that customers waited in lines that stretched onto the sidewalk and around the block. Everybody loved the wide selection and innovative flavors, including red velvet, cookie dough, and caramel macchiato. On the strength of excellent word of mouth, Crumbs opened more branches in the New York metropolitan area. As cupcake mania swept the country, Crumbs went public and expanded nationally.

Food trends come and go, however, and failure to anticipate change can be fatal in any business. When the cupcake craze lost steam, Crumbs was unprepared. The fickle public began moving on to the next new thing, but the bakery did not diversify its product line to include other bakery choices. As the long lines of waiting customers disappeared, the losses mounted. Crumbs closed its doors, filed for bankruptcy, and was eventually acquired by an investment partnership.

No Longer Addictive

Smartphones get smarter all the time. Innovation is a constant, and it takes a lot to stay on top. Not long ago, BlackBerry was the most coveted cell phone in the United States, with an almost cult-like following of devotees who proudly referred to themselves as "CrackBerry addicts." Today, most of BlackBerry's former enthusiasts have kicked the habit.

BlackBerry's decline was sudden and steep. On the way down, management did everything but think to win. Importantly, they never saw the big picture or connected the dots to properly assess the market dynamics. The company was so convinced of the appeal and power of its superior hardware—the actual BlackBerry mobile unit with its built-in keypad—that it completely underestimated the importance and appeal of encouraging the development of applications. The then struggling Apple company saw its importance as a key to future growth.

To add to its poor judgment, BlackBerry also downplayed the value of individual consumers, preferring to focus on large corporate accounts and bulk sales. As a result individual users were soon making their way to iPhone, Android, and others that focused on engaging the individual user with smartly designed hardware plus a vast array of apps. Today BlackBerry commands less than 3 percent of the U.S. market and is struggling to stay afloat.

These examples of successes and failures offer compelling evidence of the effectiveness and need for Think to Win and the TTW approach. When leaders think to win and invest in enhancing the thinking capability of their people, individuals at all levels and in more functions are more willing to contribute. Moreover, the quality of what they offer improves. TTW gives them new analytical skills, making their insights more relevant and more valuable. People take ownership; they take pride. They feel good about being part of an organization that has a bright future, a place that encourages them to step up, and a place where they can see they are making a difference. TTW becomes part of the new culture that represents ongoing success.

It's a funny thing about success—it's habit forming. Success becomes something to be expected, something people begin to count on and invest in—financially and personally. Attitudes and behaviors change when employees at all levels share a common belief that their organization is an exciting and fulfilling place to be. Everyone brings their best self to work, and the organization thrives.

That's a key reason we're passionate about Think to Win. It changes not just organizations, but individuals. Structured yet flexible, TTW grabs the power inherent in asking the right questions, focuses that energy on what matters most, and harnesses it to find solutions. In the process, we think you'll become excited, engaged, and energized.

How do you begin Think to Win? We have assembled everything you need. In the next chapter, we start detailing the principles and step-by-step process that define TTW. We will also show you how to use TTW tools and frameworks and give useful examples of how TTW works in real time. We invite you to come with us as we unleash the power of Think to Win and put that power in your hands. We assure you that you'll be surprised and excited by how quickly TTW changes your thinking and the results you'll achieve. So let's get started.

Principles for Winning

Think to Win (TTW) is more than a process or set of tools. It's a mindset that becomes habitual. It's a way of looking at all aspects of life—both professional and personal—problems as well as opportunities, big issues, and small nagging concerns. TTW can be mastered by everyone and used throughout a lifetime. And everything you need to know is in this book.

We start with five principles that serve as our compass to keep us focused and guide us to concentrate on what matters. Our principles are the foundation of Think to Win. They're integral to every step in the process and we'll refer to them often as we make our way through TTW.

Here they are:

- ▶ Challenge assumptions
- ▶ Scope the issue
- ▶ Rely on facts and data
- ▶ Focus on the vital few
- ▶ Connect the dots

And here's what they mean and why they are so important.

Challenge Assumptions

An open mind is essential for Think to Win and it starts with a clean slate that accepts nothing is a given. Many of our assumptions are so basic that we accept them without even realizing it. There must be a willingness, and even an eagerness, to identify, explore, and reimagine all of them. Understanding our assumptions is the starting point for putting TTW to work whether we're trying to solve a problem or take advantage of an opportunity.

The importance of this understanding is a lesson Jill shared with her board of directors soon after she became CEO of a large New England nonprofit. The 22 communities served by the organization depended heavily on the nonprofit's 600 employees for affordable daycare, after-school enrichment programs, and scholarships for children to attend summer camps.

Early in her tenure, however, Jill faced a financial crisis so serious the nonprofit's continued existence was in doubt. Expenditures were crippling the organization. The primary source of the hemorrhaging was the high cost of maintaining a number of expensive properties. Some had been bought years earlier; others had been bequeathed by donors. Upkeep was preventing the nonprofit from helping more kids. But the structures on the properties were considered sacred cows, and any proposal to sell them was taboo. The unspoken assumption was that these buildings defined and identified the organization with its constituents—and especially with its influential corporate donor committee.

To address the financial crisis, Jill engaged her board and executive staff in the TTW process. Jill needed to set priorities that would improve the short-term financial picture and establish a framework for long-term viability. The members of the board represented a cross section of ages, genders, and ethnicities, and reflected how deeply the organization was integrated into the community. There were business executives, lawyers, elected officials, shop owners, educators, and parents. As the board began to look at the issues, Jill emphasized that "Challenge all assumptions" was the mantra for the first session—everything was on the table, including the buildings.

Were the structures really necessary? If the organization had no buildings, would it still be able to serve the community? These questions were no longer taboo.

Several intense days of lively and forthright debate followed. Members of the board and staff looked closely at the organization's values and what its work meant to the community. They all agreed that the nonprofit must remain true to its service organization mission, which they defined as developing and supporting strong children, strong families, and a strong community in spirit, mind, and body. Buildings were just venues. Essential services to the community defined the organization, not its real estate.

This fundamental understanding changed the direction of the organization and energized the staff and the board members. Together they developed a new plan that reimagined how the nonprofit served the community and laid the groundwork for how it would continue in the future. They made the decision to sell off some properties and focus their financial resources on much-needed repairs and upgrades to those they retained. The nonprofit is now stronger than ever, and there is a new spirit of enthusiasm throughout the organization.

CHALLENGING ASSUMPTIONS

"But we've always done it that way!" Do you feel like screaming when you hear this? Or at the very least, rolling your eyes? The question is why do we keep hearing this? In today's world, why are so few employees willing to step up and challenge the "way we've always done it"?

Let's start by defining the concept: challenging assumptions means not only having an open mind, but also going a step further by questioning accepted beliefs and raising new concerns.

There is significant employee trepidation in challenging assumptions for a variety of reasons. Some don't know what it means, or even how to begin. Others are intimidated by a culture that emphasizes conforming to "tried and true" processes. And finally, it takes a strong individual to take a stance that disagrees with top managers.

(Continues)

However, it is possible to increase the willingness of employees to challenge existing assumptions. Research shows that with awareness and training, the willingness will increase by more than 50 percent. And employees who feel comfortable in challenging assumptions often have the same attitude in identifying new business opportunities.

Scope the Issue

TTW requires clarity of thought and discipline, even before the analytical process begins. If an issue or problem isn't properly scoped out, everyone involved spins their wheels. While TTW can be applied at *any* level or scale, it is important to identify and agree upon the scope of application. Within a company, is the scope of the issue departmental, divisional, or companywide? Agreeing on the appropriate scope helps align everyone to work from the same page.

One of the biggest caveats is the importance of avoiding "scope creep." If an issue or problem isn't properly scoped, then wasted time, energy, and resources are sure to result.

Hank knew the importance of scope when he took over as vice president of operations for a small appliance manufacturer. He was told that the company's "manufacturing process was broken" and needed a "complete overhaul." But complete overhauls are costly and time consuming, and Hank also knew that he had very little of either to get things fixed.

So rather than plunge headlong into a multiteam, multiphased overall study, Hank spent a few days observing and asking questions. His observations pointed to problems with the engineering work that preceded the manufacturing process. A spotlight on the engineering function was much more focused, manageable, and easier to work with and fix. So time spent scoping an issue is well spent . . . and imperative. Being able to define what has to be addressed in one or two crisp sentences is critical for success.

TRY THIS

Put the Writing on the Wall

Ask your team to pinpoint the scale of the issue. Is it departmental? Companywide? Structural? Functional? Identify the problem as specifically as possible. Put it in writing. Post it on the wall for everyone to see. Rework it until everyone agrees.

SCOPE AND SCALE

Bestselling author and consultant Tony Schwartz talks about the iPhone prayer. Have you ever seen the iPhone prayer in action? It is used to describe a posture assumed by users of an iPhone or another hand-held device in an effort to use that device in a discreet manner. This is usually done while the person is in a meeting or attending an important function. It involves grasping the device between the hands in a prayer position in an attempt to shield the display screen's glow, while the user's head is bowed down with shoulders hunched over. Sound familiar?

One of the simplest, but most important, management principle is the ability to communicate. But a common issue is that in the business environment, management fails to communicate effectively, especially in defining the scope of an issue. The dimension of *scope* is defined as "determining the appropriate *scope of analysis* to address the right issues within your control." So how can we apply this in communicating within a business environment?

When faced with defining a problem, think first about the scale of the issue. For someone in high levels of management, it might require organization-wide communication. For sales, it might only be the sales function.

Our research shows that just over 35 percent of the survey respondents were able to clearly and consistently define the most significant business issues facing them. If you can't define

(Continues)

the problem with the right scaled approach and the appropriate scope, you may be solving "world hunger" when only the hours of operation for the cafeteria need to be changed. When the principles of scope were applied, there was a 42 percent increase in the awareness of the issues that needed to be addressed.

Rely on Facts and Data

Anecdotes are not data. Facts define an issue in a way that leads to meaningful, valid conclusions that anecdotes, instinct, and gut feelings can never do. Do we have enough data? Do we have too much and can't tell what really matters? How confident are we in the integrity of our "facts"? We may want to hear from people who think "going with their gut" is the right approach, but we always have to keep in mind that facts can never be ignored.

And we don't want to just compile facts; we want to know what they really mean. Let's say that our product has a 75 percent market share. This means that we're doing great, right? Not necessarily. Not if our share last year was 90 percent. What if our market is changing drastically? And what do we mean by "market"? Are we acting like Blockbuster, clinging to brick-and-mortar stores and fatally underestimating the Netflix impact on our future? To put it another way, are we resting easy because we have 75 percent of the buggy whip market even as the new Model Ts are rolling off the assembly line?

TTW means that we must avoid the temptation to mistake assumptions for evidence and that we must be rigorous in separating empirical data from "common knowledge." "Common knowledge" is sometimes neither, and things that "everyone knows" are not always correct. The maxim used to be: *When in doubt, go with something tried and true.* We believe the saying now should be: *If it's old and tried, it's probably no longer true.*

Keep in mind that people who argue best aren't always right. Drama majors may be able to talk rings around airline mechanics; this doesn't mean that they know more about why the starboard engine is overheating. Listeners tend to give more credence to points of view that are passionately or eloquently expressed. When those opinions and beliefs are not grounded in fact, they can lead to faulty analysis, or immobilize decision makers at a time when bold action is called for.

TRY THIS

Get Rid of Sloppy Writing to Get Rid of Sloppy Thinking

Opinion and common knowledge hide in the passive voice. Be ruthless in eliminating it. Rewrite phrases such as "It is said that . . ." to make it clear who is doing the saying, and why they are justified in saying it. Drive for clarity in any opinion-based statements. Buttress value judgment descriptors—words or phrases like best, most popular, *and* greatest*—with statistical evidence. Avoid superlatives that can't be nailed down. The claim that any beverage is "the world's most refreshing" has no more validity than the hyperbolic contention that any guy is "the most interesting man in the world."*

The recent economic recession propelled a well-known furniture manufacturer into a dramatic downsizing. But even after the cuts, market conditions remained sluggish, and the company's future remained precarious. In an effort to address the problem, top managers hosted a town hall forum for middle and upper management in order to elicit feedback on additional belt-tightening measures that they believed were needed. They were taken aback by the response. Some department heads were so opposed and vociferously negative about any further downswing that they abandoned their plan, choosing instead to ride out the situation and hoping conditions would improve.

The leaders were afraid their top talent would jump ship if any major changes were implemented. Each time restructuring and a new direction for the company were raised over the next 18 months, the leaders caved, even though they were convinced that change was needed. As the company's performance tumbled from bad to worse, the CEO and chief human resources officer finally decided they needed facts. Some quick research was imperative and what they found shocked them:

▶ On a 10-point scale that measured how the employees felt about the clarity of the mission and future direction of the company, the score was only 2.2 out of 10.

▶ Rather than being averse to change and restructuring, the organization overwhelmingly craved it. In fact, top talent was poised to leave if leadership failed to act.

The result was fast action and a solid turnaround, based on a fact-based plan and not on the protests of a handful of discontents.

FACTS VERSUS OPINIONS

"In my opinion, I feel we should pursue option 1 because everyone in the room knows that Category A is better than Category B!" How many times have you heard that or something similar in a meeting? How much better would it be to say something like, "During 2014, sales have surged 14 percent, based primarily on the launch of new product XYZ, which clearly demonstrates that option 1, focused on building sales in the value sector, is the clear choice for the long-term success of our company."

The dimension of facts versus opinions uses data to make decisions and reach meaningful, valid conclusions. Opinions and conjecture do not provide accurate support for decision making. It is essential that you have the ability to discriminate between facts and opinions so you will be able to make effective, fact-based recommendations.

And that may sound easy, but our research has shown that only 47 percent of the respondents thought that people in their organization were effective in discriminating between fact and opinion.

There is clearly a need to move away from opinion and increase data-based decision making. So how do we demonstrate progress?

Focus on the clarity of the words used in a discussion and question when someone uses words like, "most," "all," or "none," or says, "Everyone knows that . . . ," stop and ask for the facts that support the statement. By doing so, we have been able to demonstrate a 53 percent increase in avoiding conjecture by employing facts when making decisions.

Focus on the Vital Few

When faced with a company, operating unit, or department that is mired in problems, the best approach is to identify them all and attack them all. Right?

We think not.

TRY THIS

Start Big

Beginning with a daunting list of issues is fine, as long as you narrow it down. Write them all on a large piece of paper. Can you identify a theme or pattern? Group the patterns and take another look. What would happen if several of the items—or even several of the groups— were not addressed right away? What would happen if they were never addressed at all? Answering these questions will go a long way toward focusing on the vital few that really matter.

Although there may be an instinctual desire to solve problems by waging an attack on all fronts, this type of scattershot approach rarely yields the best results. Rather than scoring multiple victories, the process of spreading resources to cover more territory generally makes them less effective, and usually results in a failure to make significant progress on the vital few priorities that really matter.

When Rita took on the task of revitalizing a once-popular energy drink line, it was in freefall. The brand had lost critical shelf space in key markets, elbowed out by aggressive competition from a newly introduced brand backed by strong, youth-oriented ad campaigns. Market share had plunged from 40 percent to 28 percent in less than a year. Leadership feared this was a death spiral and was threatening to cut its losses by discontinuing the product line. Rita's colleagues saw the brand as stale and irrelevant and did not believe that she would be able to resuscitate it, no matter what she did.

But Rita took up the challenge. As she conducted her initial review, she was impressed by the quality and quantity of research the prior team had collected. It had amassed a huge amount of data on consumer needs, demographics, and changing consumption patterns. The prior team identified a long list of problems that needed fixing, all of which it tried to tackle simultaneously. Not surprisingly, it failed. Trying to stretch limited resources to cover multiple initiatives resulted in an anemic effort that produced no wins and a lot of frustration. It also resulted in the departure of Rita's predecessor.

You may be familiar with the Pareto Principle, better known as the 80-20 rule—the idea that roughly 20 percent of the causes generate about 80 percent of the effects. The rule is named for Vilfredo Pareto, a turn-of-the-century Italian engineer-economist-sociologist-philosopher, who noticed that 20 percent of the pea pods in his garden yielded 80 percent of the peas.

In today's competitive environment, we're way beyond pea pods, so TTW has given Pareto an upgrade: the 80-20 rule has become the 90-10 rule. With TTW, we believe that pinpointing the most important 10 percent will impact about 90 percent of the whole. This applies to both problems and opportunities, and this is what Rita did with her team.

To winnow down her predecessor's long list of problems, Rita conducted a key issues workshop. She asked her team members to arrive at a consensus list of no more than six priority issues—the vital few. Then, by applying criteria such as competitive threats, consumer choices, pricing, customer requirements, and category growth, they sliced the list in half, pruning it down to the three that were most critical, two of which needed urgent attention.

The biggest of those was pricing. The price gap between Rita's prestige brand and the rest of the competition had grown so large that many consumers had decided it was no longer worth the money. As with the Duracell Ultra battery, even customers who believed Rita's energy drink was "better" didn't think it was "sufficiently better" to warrant its significantly higher cost.

Rita knew that she had to confront the issue head-on; no baby steps would do. She had to sharply cut the price of her energy drink and do so immediately. A week later, during a presentation to her division leadership, Rita laid out the vital few initiatives her team had identified, with a price reduction as her number one priority. Rita's boss liked her decisiveness; she also liked the clarity of thought behind it. Within six months, Rita's energy drink line started to regain market share. A year later, the company greenlighted an innovative ad campaign to accelerate the brand's resurgence.

FOCUS ON THE VITAL FEW

Have you ever worked in an organization that seemed to always have a "laundry list" of key initiatives, but no vision of how to get from here to there?

You are not alone. Many companies have a problem in communicating business goals, prioritizing agendas and designing strategies that target specific key issues through clear and concise practices.

The dimension of the vital few focuses on those issues that should be addressed versus tackling everything.

Before you begin a project, think about the following:

- ► Do I thoroughly understand the issues?
- ► Can I identify which issues are most important?
- ► How can I prioritize which ones to go after?

Employees can learn this competency by learning to correctly write issues, breaking them down into conclusions and implications and beginning to introduce action language into implications.

(Continues)

In fact, our research has shown that employees self-report a 99 perent increase in their ability to focus on the vital few and being able to streamline from many to a few key issues after the appropriate training.

Connect the Dots

Focus is great. As Rita's experience showed, it's important to lock in on the "vital few" things that matter. But a focus that is too narrow has another name, tunnel vision, and it can blind us to the significance of the final TTW principle: linkage. If the three laws of real estate are location, location, location, for TTW they are *linkage, linkage, linkage*.

There must be a clear line of sight between problem identification and actions to be taken. Making 10,000 widgets an hour may meet an ambitious production target, but unless it also supports the broader target of achieving low-cost leadership, the accomplishment won't count for much. And if the market can't absorb all those widgets, it means even less.

This was the case for Gary, the new manager of an automotive parts plant that was considered the crown jewel of his company. Newly fitted out with the latest robotic technology, the plant should have been a low-cost/high-efficiency production star. Instead, the factory had become a notorious underachiever. Malfunctions and cost overruns were the norm, not the exception. These big and persistent problems were inflating costs, placing the company at an ever-increasing competitive disadvantage.

Gary's challenge: control costs and get the factory working efficiently. As he listened to his department heads, he spotted a common problem: they were all focused on their quotas. Not one of them was looking beyond internal production targets. When Gary studied the printouts, he saw that the state-of-the-art robotics that should have lowered production costs had actually created the problem. The newly installed equipment required a particular skill set, but the requisite workforce retraining had never taken place. As a result, technology had outpaced the capability and competence of the people on the line, which meant mistakes, downtime for the equipment, and high levels of unacceptable end product.

When Gary realized the problem, the solution was clear: improve the technical capability and competence of the work-force, and develop process improvements to boost equipment reliability, reduce rejects, and create a lower inventory level. The new plan was put in place and within six months, costs came down by 30 percent. The effect of linkage—the ability to simply connect the dots—can be very powerful and very effective.

TRY THIS

Draw a Picture

Get out the markers and colored pencils and a big piece of paper. It's time to connect the dots—literally. List problems or issues on one side, using a different color for each one. List actions to be taken on the other—color coded by which problems they address.

Do you have problems with no solutions? Do you have solutions with no problems? Are you having trouble figuring out what color some of the solutions should be?

The answers to these questions should offer clues about how to strengthen the connections in your analysis.

Let's see how these principles and the TTW process worked at one iconic company. When Rob DeMartini took over in 2008 as CEO of the sporting goods favorite New Balance, the company was at a crossroads. For a number of years, sales were stagnant and the bottom line also suffered. Rob believed he could provide charismatic leadership. He also felt his management team had many star performers. But the company needed something more.

The company had to learn to think and act differently. So his first order of business was to introduce Think to Win for developing a place that would reignite growth. He had to lead his senior executive team through a disciplined and rigorous approach that would move New Balance from a great running shoe, *product-focused* company to a *brand company* that was focused on great running shoes and beyond.

LINKAGE . . . LINKAGE . . . LINKAGE

What are the three laws of TTW? We all know the adage that the three laws of real estate are: "location, location, and location." There is a similar law for organizational strategy, namely: "linkage, linkage, linkage."

Linkage is one of the most important concepts to understand. It provides a line of sight and ensures accountability within an organization. However, our research shows that 65 percent of the employees surveyed indicated that their projects were neither directly linked nor aligned to the corporation's strategy. For an organization to be effective, linkage between the overall goals of the organization and the project plans are essential. With training, "project plans tied to strategies with clear accountability" increased by over 68 percent.

"Marketing the brand was something New Balance had never really done," says Rob. "We were reluctant to even stand in that competitive arena. In the past, our company leaders believed if you made a great product, everything would fall into place. But as our business got more complicated and more competitors moved into our primary distribution channel, our story wasn't getting through."

New Balance had to change its thinking and its approach to doing business. So Rob and a small team of senior managers spent time conducting a fact-based analysis of external trends and internal strengths and weaknesses. From there, they identified the most important issues to address, decided how to reposition New Balance, and made critical choices on setting a direction and positioning New Balance to achieve success.

Rob and his team started with a situation assessment of New Balance's recent past. In the early 2000s, New Balance grew rapidly in distribution channels that were far less crowded than they were at the present, importantly in the "big-box stores" such as Sports Authority and Dick's Sporting Goods. Nike was very narrowly distributed, and so New Balance had a disproportionately large market share in big box retail.

By the mid 2000s, Nike entered the big box channel. And Nike was 10 times bigger than New Balance. "All of a sudden we weren't the darling of this channel anymore; we were playing defense, fighting to tell our story with a competitor who was spending big time on marketing," Rob says.

For several years, New Balance struggled in the big box channel, a valiant David trying to beat Goliath. Badly outspent and outmuscled, New Balance's sales stagnated, and earnings eroded as it pursued its unsuccessful plan, believing that great products would win out in the end. The 100-year-old company did have great products and a great story to tell, but not enough consumers heard them above the marketing salvos coming from Nike.

For Rob and his team, several issues had to be addressed.

1. New Balance was primarily a running shoe business. Should it morph into a multisport performance brand business embodying health, youth, and activity?
2. Nike was winning in the big box channel where New Balance had previously dominated. What were New Balance's options?
3. The consumer was not hearing the New Balance story. How should it try to be heard?
4. New Balance didn't have strong relationships in the other important distribution channels . . . with the independent/specialty retailers who played an important role in the running and apparel category. Should it try to focus on them or continue to concentrate only on the high-growth big-box store channel?

As Rob and his executive team reviewed their strengths and opportunities, they could see a very different and exciting future. Rather than continuing with a futile slugfest with Nike in the big box arena, New Balance could add a new focus and shift resources to winning in the direct-to-consumer arena. New Balance could open its own stores where it could tell its compelling brand story without competitive static.

Company stores could create a "gold standard" for the marketing, merchandising, and consumer relationships. The stores wouldn't displace other channels (wholesalers and retailers). Rather they'd be a growth catalyst and model. The executive team's goal was to triple-direct to consumer sales from 8 percent of revenue to about 25 percent over the life of the growth plan. The goal was difficult but attainable because DeMartini knew it was something the organization would really "care about."

For the company store business plan to be successful, the team members realized that running shoes weren't enough; they needed apparel to add revenue that would cover overhead retail costs and make the model work. To capture the concept of the new model, they coined the new mantra, "New Balance . . . from toe-to-head." New Balance would be more than just a running shoe brand; it would be an athletic brand from head to toe.

Not really having apparel as part of the company's DNA was an issue. New Balance could grind out a new competency in apparel through a time-consuming trial-and-error approach. Or it could think differently and acquire an apparel company, which it did.

Since the direct-to-consumer model must also have an Internet direct sales component, a similar choice existed in this space. Learn and grow . . . or acquire. New Balance acquired a small but solid Internet capability.

The independent specialty store segment, which had received short shrift when New Balance was focused on the big box channel, received extra attention. Special initiatives and programs were designed to create strong bonds with New Balance and raise the company's brand profile in these stores.

So New Balance's new thinking was employing all the principles of *Think to Win*. Old concepts and ways of doing things were challenged. The basis for new decisions was a fact-based and rigorous analysis of strengths, weaknesses, opportunities, and threats. All elements of the new thinking were tied together. And priorities were narrow and focused.

To provide even more focus, Rob and his team agreed on what they termed the "three truths." These truths encapsulated sustaining the competitive advantages that truly differentiated New Balance:

1. New Balance is first and foremost a *running brand*. The running shoe anchors everything about our brand and enables us to expand into the lifestyle arena of apparel and other merchandise.

But we must never lose focus on our running shoe heritage and brand.

2. New Balance is American. Twenty-five percent of New Balance shoes are manufactured in U.S.-based factories. New Balance is the last athletic company to operate running shoe factories in the United States. New Balance maintains 5 plants that make more shoes now than they did 20 years ago. This heritage is an immutable part of the New Balance culture. More than 90 percent of the running shoes made in the United States are made by New Balance.

3. Specialty sports retailers are special. Although large sports retailers and big-box stores are important, the footwear and running apparel business is heavily influenced and represented by over 4,000 independent family shoe stores. Those are critical to New Balance's future—its growth, its success, and its new strategically oriented business model.

Getting Results

New Balance more than doubled its stores. In the United States, it operates about 190 units and globally around 1,200. Over four years, the company has become a $3.3 billion business, growing at an above-average rate throughout. The final chapter for New Balance is yet to be written, but the prospects are excellent for more great TTW results.

While most of the illustrations and examples in this book focus on professional and business situations, TTW works very effectively with personal issues. Emma is a young professional who is looking for a new position with a different organization. She has been working as a learning and development coordinator for a small human resources firm. She hopes to find a similar position with a larger organization where she can expand her career interests and development. Like many young professionals, Emma is struggling to sort through the labyrinth of possible career opportunities. She has important choices to make, but right now she's immobilized. She doesn't know how to begin narrowing down her options. We will follow Emma's progress, chapter by chapter as she uses TTW to guide her search.

EMMA AND THE FIVE GUIDING PRINCIPLES

1. **Challenge assumptions.** Emma initially assumes she will have to confine her job search to another human resources position. But upon reviewing her skill set and experience, she finds that the fundamental elements of her career experience can translate more broadly. She decides she can look outside the HR field for positions that will allow her to apply her recent experience and take on new responsibilities to grow her skills.

2. **Scope the issue.** Geography will play an important part in her job search. In the long run, Emma thinks she would prefer to relocate to California. At present, she is living in Connecticut. Her family ties, and equally important, her network of professional connections, are centered in Connecticut. Although she will hold the idea of California as a goal for the long term, it's not now within reach. She realistically decides to narrow the scope of her search to a 200-mile radius from her current home. That gives her plenty of options in the Connecticut, Massachusetts, and New York greater metropolitan areas.

3. **Rely on facts and data.** Emma finds the prospect of looking for a new job daunting. Several well-meaning but pessimistic friends inform her that they know for certain that "there are no jobs out there." Before a defeatist attitude sets in, Emma needs to verify how true these "facts" really are. She creates a spreadsheet of possible options, and is greatly reassured to see how many possibilities exist. Yet she knows there is much more research to do.

4. **Focus on the vital few.** Emma's next task is to list what she needs to begin her job search and prioritize the list. There are over 100 organizations in the geographic area that she can pursue. As she looks at it, she realizes she not only has to consider the position, she also has to make sure she is not casting too wide a net, and must focus on the most relevant

companies. Emma begins to think about a "top 10" list. If there is a position she is really interested in, she needs to follow up and focus her energies there.

5. **Connect the dots.** When Emma looks at her first list of possibilities, she is happy there are a lot of them. But she is disappointed in the jobs themselves. The positions all look too much like the job she already had. She realizes that she is focusing too narrowly on jobs that are in her realm of direct experience. She is not paying enough attention to her research on jobs and employers where her skills can potentially be a great fit, even if the situation is completely outside the HR realm. She also realizes that she is not taking advantage of her professional network. She needs to step back and focus on her real "challenge," then link what she knows about herself and the job market to specific goals and strategies. Emma needs to make sure she "connects the dots" between her career aspirations, formal education, and training, to her goals and job search strategies.

Chapter Summary

The five guiding principles are the foundation of Think to Win and are integral to every step in the process. There's nothing difficult or mysterious about TTW; the underlying principles are straightforward and easy to access.

1. **Challenge assumptions by keeping our minds open.** We have to ask questions about why we're doing what we're doing. And conversely we must reimagine options for new or different approaches. Our assumptions may be well-grounded, but the situation may have changed or may have been altered by a shifting competitive environment, by new technology, by macroeconomic factors. The warp-speed changes of today make it more likely that assumptions must be reimagined rather than stay fixed.

2. **Scoping the issue is essential to the TTW process.** Just because the thinking is strategic doesn't mean the issue involved must be big. Regardless of its size, all issues should receive the TTW approach. Whether we're thinking about the numbers in our global workforce or the price we can charge for our customized cupcakes doesn't matter. What does matter is that we identify the precise scope of the undertaking so we can set it in the right framework and have everyone working from the same page.

3. **Facts inform outcomes.** Opinions, beliefs, biases, hunches, intuitions, gut feelings—all of these may or may not be on target. But we must realize what they are and aren't. And we must be sure that our decision making relies on fact-based analysis.

4. **Focus on the vital few.** Don't try to take on everything at once. It may make us feel like a hero, but it's more likely to undercut our chances for success than enhance them. Even if we are working with an overabundance of resources, which is not usually the case, trying to communicate and align people on multiple tasks and targets rarely works out well. Prioritizing and working on the vital few, always works best. Apply the "90-10" rule: focus on the 10 percent of actions that will deliver 90 percent of the results.

5. **Connecting the dots seems so self-evident.** But in the rush to accomplish specific tasks and goals, the need to identify linkages and ensure the connections often are overlooked. And the consequences of such oversights can be a hit to morale as well as missed opportunities. If a unit in a group believes its targets are being overlooked, or short-changed, or aren't being incorporated within the overall effort, the "second-class citizen syndrome" can easily take root.

These five principles are our *compass,* helping guide us through the TTW approach.

Chapter 2 Exercises

Here are some questions and exercises to guide you in applying the TTW principles. As you spend time with each of the principles, your overall competence with thinking strategically will improve. So spend the time and the results will follow.

Mastering the Five Principles

Building an organization with strategic thinking capability starts with creating a new mindset, both for yourself and for your colleagues. This mental transformation begins with our five guiding principles that lead the way in helping you think differently. They underlie every step in the TTW process.

Challenge Assumptions

Having an open mind is a necessity. It starts with an exploration of what you might be taking for granted. Peel away any built-up layers of assumptions by asking how they came to be accepted, and envisioning what would happen if they were not.

Begin by asking the *what if*? and *why*? questions:

- ▶ Why did we see the need for this decision in the past?
- ▶ What if we do things differently?
- ▶ What if our biggest competitor were in this room; what would he or she say about us?
- ▶ What if we reimagine things radically? What if we create a new market segment?
- ▶ What if I owned this business? What would I do differently?

Exercise: "From Then to Now"

Continue with the following actions:

- ▶ Ask the person in the room with the most experience to describe what the business, culture, and attitude were like when he or she first arrived.
- ▶ Progress to the next most senior person to describe differences now versus when he or she started.

- ▶ Continue to record differences as the length of service shortens.
- ▶ At the end of the exercise, ask what was learned? What if things hadn't changed? Where would we be today?

Scope the Issue

First ask at what level does the problem exist?

- ▶ Is it a companywide issue?
- ▶ Is it within my business unit?
- ▶ Is it a team and/or departmental concern?
- ▶ What is within my circle of influence? My circle of concern?
- ▶ Who is the "person" who could begin to address this issue best?
- ▶ What is within scope? What is out of scope?

Rely on Facts and Data

Meaningful decisions and conclusions are drawn from clear and precise information. Develop a heightened awareness of how to spot opinion and speculation that may be disguised as data:

- ▶ Use facts to make decisions and reach meaningful, valid conclusions.
- ▶ Drive for clarity on any opinion-based statements.
- ▶ Ask for clarity/quantification with colleagues. Words or phrases such as *best, great, competitive edge,* and *best informed* should be challenged. Always ask: What's the evidence?

Focus on the Vital Few

Thinking to win means making the deliberate choice not to tackle everything at one time. Prioritizing and working on the vital few always works best.

- ▶ Narrow conclusions down to the vital few—use the 90-10 rule.
- ▶ What are the themes coming out of your analysis?
- ▶ What did you learn?
- ▶ Which conclusions are the most important? Create a statement for each.

Connect the Dots

Thinking to win means looking both ways. There should be a clear line of sight throughout the entire process, from beginning to end. You and your colleagues need to see and understand the linkage from one step to another, both forward and backward.

▶ What informed your goals and strategies? Is there anything you learned about your competitor that is missing from your strategies?

▶ Visually show linkages between your analysis and your solutions. In your documents, color code relationships between goals and strategies and analysis.

▶ Print PowerPoint pages and align them horizontally. Can you track ideas from start to finish?

Organizational Assessment

Use the following table as a checklist for identifying TTW principles and practices. This will help you to better understand where you need to focus your energies. To get an idea of where you stand, read through each statement and jot down a rating of 1 to 5:

Concept/Process	Scale: 1 = Low, 5 = High
Challenging Assumptions: To what extent do I encourage myself and others to reimagine aspects of previous assumptions; a willingness/eagerness to challenge them and raise new issues?	
Scoping the Issue: To what extent do I articulate between function, level, or teams to address the right issues within my control?	
Facts Versus Opinions: To what extent do I consistently seek clarity on or support evidence to go beyond generalizations such as "best in our market"?	
Focusing on the Vital Few: To what extent do I consolidate my analysis into 3 themes that raise issues to address?	
Linkage: To what extent do I "connect the dots" between analysis, conclusions, implications, goals, and strategies?	

Review individual items. Look for items where you scored lower (3 and below) and think about the following questions:

- ▶ What do I believe is driving the score?
- ▶ What do I need to stop, start, or continue doing?
- ▶ What do I want the result to be?

CHAPTER 3

What It Takes
to Win

What makes for a winning team in business? A charismatic manager who inspires her team members? A superstar who can outperform everyone? An all-consuming desire to win? Or is it luck and chance—everything coming together just right for victory? All are factors, but they're not the real key.

When Michelle Stacy was given responsibility for restructuring the 500-person global professional sales group for Oral-B, the iconic dental products company, she found an organization that had lots of star performers who were eager, enthusiastic, and dedicated. But there also was virtually no consistency in strategic priorities and tactics across the globe. The commanding lead that Oral-B enjoyed in selling its products—manual and power toothbrushes, toothpastes, mouthwashes, and dental floss—and gaining patient recommendations from dentists and dental hygienists was being eroded by the very aggressive actions of Sonicare and Colgate.

Talent and persistence weren't going to be enough to win in the future. The Oral-B professional sales group (SG) had to learn how to act differently and think to win. So Michelle's first order of business was to introduce the thinking necessary to develop a strategic plan that would guide the organization to future success. She led her team through a structured approach for making decisions, a thinking process that aligned the organization and enabled its members to embrace major changes.

As we'll see later in this chapter, by using TTW, the Oral-B professional SG moved from a struggling collection of talented individuals to a coherent, coordinated team with a long-term vision and detailed action plan for success.

Principles + Process

So how do we move from knowing the right principles for winning to putting those principles to work? Understanding the principles is important. Creating a mindset that acknowledges and embraces them is requisite. But Think to Win calls for principles **plus** a process. The strength and power of TTW flow from melding the five principles into an orderly, analytical process.

To visualize the process, we use an hourglass (see Figure 3.1) that expresses many aspects of TTW. The hourglass is a clear signal that timeliness is a critical factor in our TTW approach. But it's also much more, providing an overview of the entire process that we'll look at briefly now.

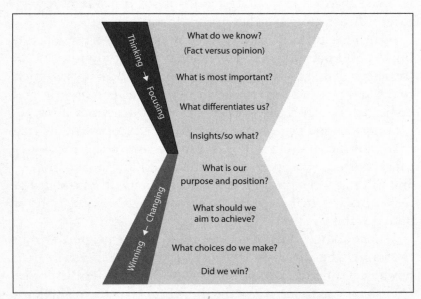

FIGURE 3.1.   HOURGLASS REPRESENTATION OF TTW.

The top half of our hourglass acts as a funnel of information. As the hourglass narrows, the questions become more specific and more focused. With each question, *we concentrate and strengthen our knowledge and understanding.* This is *convergent thinking.* In other words, a large amount of factual data is compressed into relevant parcels that can be analyzed and dissected further. We analyze, sort, and sift, and then we reanalyze, resort, and reorganize.

As we look at the hourglass (see Figure 3.1), the first thing we notice is the wide opening at the top. Through this opening, we start identifying and processing what we know about our issue, challenge, or problem. We'll be guided in deciding what facts to consider and what data to process by something called an *umbrella statement.* This is a simple statement that starts to frame our issue or problem by telling us such things as its scope and most impactful aspects.

We get additional guidance with our *frameworks*, which are tools that help us place data into buckets. They're an important part of the discipline and structure. We provide a blueprint for creating customized frameworks to handle specific needs as well as offering several existing formats that have been proven to be broadly successful over time. We want our fact base and data gathering to be robust, but we don't want to be paralyzed by an overload of data. And our frameworks keep everything manageable. (For details on frameworks and other tools, look at the exercises at the end of this chapter.)

As we answer the questions, we add meaning and significance to important facts and jettison less critical information. We *converge* on what really matters and look for *insights* that will have *implications* for how we should proceed. At this stage, we aren't looking for detailed, quantified conclusions. We want a short list of observations and understandings—*key issues*—that tell us where the data are pointing.

With this key issues list, we move from *convergent* to *divergent thinking.* The list provides the basis for goal setting, which then goes through a series of steps that takes the TTW process to its action phase. The bottom half of the hourglass is where we address our issues, set our *objectives* and *goals*, identify possible *strategies* and alternative courses of actions, make choices from among them, identify *initiatives*—actions for implementing *strategies*—and determine how we will measure our success. When we reach the bottom of the hourglass, we have *key messages* that summarize what we know, what we're going to do, and what the impact will be.

This is just a brief overview of the TTW process flow, which is further outlined in Figure 3.2. So don't worry if terms and concepts aren't crystal clear. We come back to them and provide more details and illustrations in each chapter. And as we move through the chapters, the simplicity and power of each step in this TTW process is likely to surprise you.

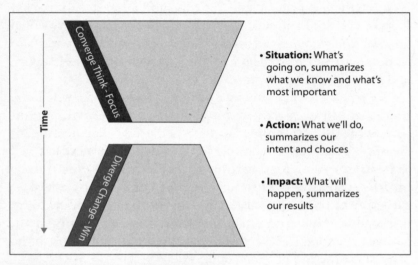

FIGURE 3.2.   TTW PROCESS FLOW.

Umbrella Statements

Let's look now at the first question we ask at the start of the TTW process: *What are we trying to solve? What's our issue?* We call the answer to this question our *umbrella statement*. And it's critically important to make this statement precise, concise, and something agreed to by everyone involved.

Top executive Gary Cohen says this sounds easy; but it's not: "Throughout my career, I've worked on iconic consumer brands, including Gillette, Oral-B, Playtex, Hawaiian Tropic, and Timex. In each of these environments, getting people to actually agree on the situation [the umbrella statement] sounds so simple. But it's one of the biggest barriers companies have in making the right choices. A lot of the issues that need to get solved are not at the 30,000 foot level; they are not 'where-do-I-take-this-company' issues. They are 'what-choices-do-I-make-day-to-day? issues." Yet in Gary's experience, too many individuals, teams, or even executive committees will construct broad, encompassing umbrella statements that make it impossible to formulate actionable plans.

In our experience, there are often *no efforts* made to create an umbrella statement. People are so eager to get to a solution that they overlook the definition phase of the process. Or they assume that everyone has the same understanding and definition of the issue so there's no need to discuss it. Yet whenever we work with teams or groups within companies and go around the table asking each person to give his or her view of the issue, there is never consensus or anything remotely close to common agreement.

So umbrella statements are essential. They don't have to cover an entire company or involve macro issues. Rather they have to be directly applicable to a specific issue and the specific group that's involved with it. As the beverage maker Keurig was gearing up to enter the home-brewed coffee market, its engineering team had to ensure that there was an adequate supply of single-serving brew cups. So it developed this concise, compelling statement:

> The beverage system is projected to grow significantly over the next few years. Continuous supply of K-Cups is critical to the brewing system's success. We need to develop a packaging equipment supply chain strategy to ensure highly reliable, efficient, and cost-effective equipment is available for our brewing partners.

Gary says that another common problem is the failure to reach agreement on the umbrella statement. Without this alignment, any approach that emerges from the process will be doomed to failure.

How clearly we define our umbrella statement goes a long way toward determining how successful we will be in addressing it. To unleash the power of TTW, our first task is to answer several challenging questions:

- ▶ *What* defines the issue?
- ▶ *Why* are we dealing with our issue? What happens if we don't?
- ▶ *Who* is involved with this issue? Who is "under the umbrella" with us? Why is this issue important to them? Can we get their buy-in and align them on our umbrella statement?

When working with members of groups, we spend a lot of time urging them to gain agreement on the umbrella statement. Collective commitment is very powerful. We work and rework the umbrella statement, honing the concept, weighing the words carefully, building and reinforcing agreement among participants as we go. Securing *alignment*—getting people on the same page at the start—saves more time and conflict than any other single step in TTW.

This doesn't mean that it's easy to get everyone to agree. In our workshops, we give each participant a piece of flip chart paper. We ask participants to write down their thoughts; then we put all the papers up on the wall. Some participants try to *boil the ocean*. They identify a problem that is too vast; it's outside their area of control and far too big to solve. Others think too small—they choose insignificant, marginal issues that would have no real impact. Gaining consensus on the true issue is a challenge when working with these extremes.

Strong Statements—Convey Tension and Underscore Conviction

Let's see what's involved in preparing an effective umbrella statement. We have found that they contain several attributes:

- ▶ **Clear.** An umbrella statement should be succinct, not long and detailed. Two or three clear, declarative sentences should be written so people can understand the statement without further explanation.

▶ **Focused.** An umbrella statement must be specific to the organization and to the situation at hand. An effective statement focuses on a single problem.

▶ **Compelling.** An umbrella statement should identify the importance of an issue and the consequences of not taking action. The statement should convey tension and underscore the conviction that something must be done.

What are some characteristics of ineffective umbrella statements? They are vague and sound as if they could apply to anyone in any organization at any time. If statements don't create a compelling sense of urgency, they tend to be ignored.

Here are examples of effective and ineffective statements. The first involves a magazine publisher whose subscription levels have been declining. As a result, ad revenues also have dropped:

> **Ineffective.** Our circulation has been declining because our subscribers have been moving to e-readers and phone apps.
>
> **Effective.** The landscape we operate in has changed dramatically. We are challenged by competitors who provide information to our consumers for free. Not only are we losing customers, but we are in danger of becoming obsolete.

Now consider the issue facing the design team for a personal care products company. Its largest retail customer (30 percent of the business) has demanded improved display packaging for the holiday season. It has to be easy for store clerks to handle and very eye-catching to consumers in the aisles. Only one vendor will be chosen:

> **Ineffective.** Merchandising is an important part of our business. We do not have the optimal solution in place for our product lines. Unless we completely change the way we package our products, we will be at a competitive disadvantage.
>
> **Effective.** Smart Stores has challenged us to provide an innovative merchandising system to display our personal care products in-store during the holiday season. If we are not their vendor of choice, our sales loss will be crippling.

EMMA'S UMBRELLA ISSUE

A lot of the challenge in crafting an umbrella issue is knowing where to begin. Having looked at the five guiding principles to help her refine her approach, Emma now needs to state clearly what she is trying to accomplish.

"At this point in my professional career, I have a general sense of what I see myself doing next. Although the job market is not ideal, I must determine how I can progress my career and land a position with a northeast company that allows me to use my skills, enjoy my work, and continue to grow personally and professionally."

With this understanding of the TTW process, let's see how the Oral-B professional sales group used the five TTW principles, structured hourglass approach, and umbrella statement to reverse its stumble in the U.S. market and create a coordinated global unit that helped Oral-B drive accelerated sales growth.

Michelle and her team began by scoping the umbrella statement. From data already on hand, it became clear that the professional SG was a talented global organization whose ability to secure professional recommendations and endorsements from dentists and dental hygienists significantly impacted the purchase of manual and power toothbrushes in every major market where Oral-B operated. (In markets like Japan and Korea where it had no presence, sales suffered.)

This was the good news, but the list of concerns was lengthy, including an unclear understanding by the SG members of their real roles and responsibilities. There were no best practices, for example, that spelled out which of the 167,000 dentists and 110,000 hygienists in North America the 300 plus SG members should visit and how frequent those visits should be.

"We looked at call coverage across the world," Michelle says. "How many dental offices in each marketplace were being called on, the number of calls we were making per year, and how efficient they were. We could see there was a vast difference in how often and what the call practices were in each marketplace relative to the United States where we had a detailed understanding of the right call practice.

"We had a very inconsistent approach across the world, even in marketplaces where dental practices were similar. We should have had a similar call practice, but we didn't. We also didn't have a similar way of looking at dental schools and dental hygiene schools and how many we should visit and how often we should visit them."

There was no research that confirmed the best staffing levels, the best spending levels for marketing materials or for product sampling, and the right mix of activities to undertake. Despite the SG's importance and its positioning as a global organization, within the SG it was pretty much every man and woman for himself or herself.

Assembling more facts and data marks the next phase of TTW (Figure 3.3), which addresses the umbrella statement by answering the question: What do we know? It is important to cast a wide net for information that is the basis for what is called a situation assessment.

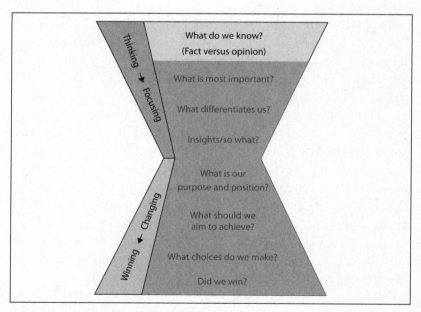

FIGURE 3.3.   WHAT DO WE KNOW?

Michelle and her team established a clear umbrella statement: *The SG's inconsistent approaches around the world and the lack of clarity about roles and responsibilities were undermining Oral-B's marketplace performance, allowing key competitors to make gains at Oral-B's expense. Without a clear global vision that provided the basis for well-defined practices and responsibilities, further losses would increase and steepen.* So they began putting together a situation assessment.

As they started, Michelle and her team used one of the TTW frameworks, known as the seven Cs. The TTW frameworks are invaluable aids that enable us to initially chunk or compartmentalize facts and later assess their meaning and relevance by viewing them within a broader context. The seven Cs are: category, company, customer, consumer, community, colleagues, and competitors.

We won't go through all the Cs, but let's briefly review some of the findings. Oral-B SG's *category* of dental professionals around the world was huge with 1.3 million in the top markets of Europe, Latin America, Asia Pacific, Africa, and the Middle East. Each market was segmented into clusters based on their estimated profit potential. Argentina, Chile, and South Africa, for example, were markets that were being *invested in for results*. The United States, United Kingdom, Germany, and Brazil were markets where the SG had to *win the battle*, while China, India, and Turkey were areas for "*testing the waters*." While Oral-B's professional sales revenue was close to $100 million in North America and nearly $20 million in the rest of the world, only North America was profitable with a margin of 25 percent. The rest of the world ran at a loss.

The *customers* were diverse consisting of key opinion leaders, academic associations, specialty dentists, and general practitioners. The approaches to reach them involved a complex marketing model that used many marketing tactics—everything from direct mail, sampling, and waiting room materials to association sponsorships, guest lecture boards, symposia, and communications to dentists and hygienists. Emphasis and use of the different tactics varied widely with most tactics randomly applied across different geographies, and many resources were misdirected.

Consumer impact, detailed by country, invariably was impressive. For example, the percentage of Oral-B's purchases influenced by dental recommendations was more than 50 percent in the United States; nearly 30 percent in the United Kingdom, Canada, and Germany; and mid 20 percent in Italy, Spain, and Australia.

Company process, systems, and structures were both limited and inconsistent. The ratio of headquarters and regional management to field workers was very low. And in the regional offices that covered Asia Pacific, Latin America, Africa, and the Middle East, there were no dedicated managers. "You had this big organization that everybody thought was valuable hidden in all sorts of unusual places in the P&L with no real way to actually understand who they were and what they were doing," says Michelle.

"And there was virtually no headquarters support. People around the world were placed in different structures with virtually no management support. You had one or two field people in every one of the global markets, sometimes 10 or 11, on their own, doing their own thing, creating their own marketing materials. There was a tremendous amount of duplication of effort and messaging."

While Oral-B headquarters had a global strategy for its business, the then current professional process varied greatly from those guidelines in its actual local tactics and execution.

As it looked at *competitors*, it noted that while Oral-B had a significant professional force, on average, it was smaller than the key competitors in the top markets.

This represents a very small portion of the total fact base gathered by Michelle and her team. The robust data prepared them for the next phase of the TTW process—preparing a SWOT analysis.

EMMA: WHAT DOES SHE KNOW?

Emma excels at technical writing, which is definitely a strength. So is her fluency in Arabic. Her father is a government employee who was posted to the Middle East during her childhood. On the other hand, she is shy and soft spoken, and often reluctant to express a strong opinion, especially if it contradicts a view presented by a boss, or even a colleague. These weaknesses could contribute to her making a poor impression during face-to-face interviews. Looking at the right or external side of the matrix (Figure 3.4), Emma might uncover an opportunity by networking through her

(Continues)

college placement office, or with other recent alumni. In contrast, however, there is a potentially serious threat out there that makes her job search more difficult. Emma needs to be concerned about the growing number of recent HR graduates who might be competing with her for a position. She can't stop the flow of graduates, of course, but she does need to make it clear how and why she would be a superior candidate.

Emma knows she must assess her situation: both internally (herself) and externally (the job market). To organize the information she has available, she creates her own framework and begins to sort her data:

- ▶ Internal (education, work experience and accomplishments, training skills, her network)
- ▶ External (job market, employers' size and reputation, culture, who she is competing with)

Doing this allows her to clearly identify her strengths, weaknesses, along with the marketplace opportunities, and threats.

Moving from assembling facts and data to culling them and assessing what's most important (see Figure 3.4) is the next phase of TTW. The importance of facts is largely determined by tying them back to their relevance in addressing the umbrella statement. Not everything we know helps in this effort.

In a *SWOT analysis*, the *S* and *W* look inward at strengths and weaknesses. Both relate to conditions within the company (or even individuals). The *O* and *T* look outward at opportunities and threats coming from beyond. The SWOT framework is organized into quadrants within a matrix (Figure 3.5) with positive factors at the top, and negative factors below. For strengths, we attempt to answer the questions: *What do we do as well or better than our competitors? What enables us to outperform our competitors?* For weaknesses, *What can we improve? What are our resource, service, or product shortcomings?* When we look outside at opportunities, we ask and answer: *What external trends*

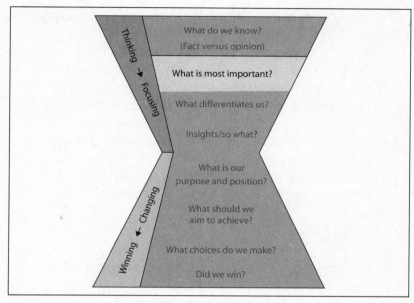

FIGURE 3.4.   WHAT IS MOST IMPORTANT?

or conditions can we (or our competitors) capitalize on? Could new technology improve our performance? And for threats: What trends or conditions should worry us? Are new competitors entering our markets? Are demographics changing?

	Internal	External
	Strengths	**Opportunities**
Positives	What do we do well?	What external trends or conditions can we or the competition capitalize on?
	Weaknesses	**Threats**
Negatives	What can we improve?	What external trends or conditions should we be wary of?

FIGURE 3.5.   SWOT FRAMEWORK.

Working from their seven Cs data, Michelle's team members filled in SWOT. The strengths were impressive:

- ▶ Dental sales professionals significantly impact consumer purchases in power and manual toothbrushes.
- ▶ Oral-B leads in use and recommendations by dentists in most markets.
- ▶ Oral-B was acknowledged for its strong leadership position in clinical brushing research.
- ▶ Professional sales activities were partially self-funding.
- ▶ Oral-B was a strong trusted brand.

And there was a list of weaknesses:

- ▶ Programs and practices were inconsistently applied across regions.
- ▶ Management of professionals was deficient.
- ▶ Roles, responsibilities, and priorities were unclear on securing recommendations versus selling products.
- ▶ Product sampling was limited.

The external trends served up several opportunities:

- ▶ Consumers trust branded products in the oral care category.
- ▶ Dentists and hygienists significantly affect the purchase of power toothbrushes.
- ▶ The power toothbrush business is in underdeveloped markets.
- ▶ Increased demand for dental care in developing markets.

Competitive threats also were strong:

- ▶ Sonicare was aggressively expanding its professional group globally.
- ▶ Competitors such as Colgate could better leverage their reputation for excellence in toothpastes, mouthwashes, and other product categories.
- ▶ Acquisitions and consolidations were likely.

We return to Michelle's story in the next chapter, but let's look now at a SWOT analysis for a different type of organization, a not-for-profit organization—an inner city charter school. Its SWOT analysis might look something like what's shown in Table 3.1.

TABLE 3.1.   SWOT ANALYSIS OF INNER CITY SCHOOL

Internal	External
Strengths	*Opportunities*
▶ Constant self-reflection and improvement ▶ Work with challenging students ▶ Build processes over time around key priorities ▶ Attract strong teachers ▶ Build collaborative structures	▶ Community support for new teaching models ▶ Still lots of popular and press support for charter schools ▶ Growing awareness of early childhood (pre-K, home care) needs ▶ New Department of Education facilities now available for expansion by state law
Weaknesses	*Threats*
▶ Too many priorities ▶ Poor communication among levels of stakeholders at times ▶ Last minute planning in the name of being nimble and responsive ▶ The coteaching model is expensive	▶ Continuous changes in regulations ▶ Technology changes in community typically behind the schools ▶ Elected officials change every two years making it difficult to keep sponsors ▶ Competition for shrinking philanthropy pool is intense

Getting It Right

Poorly done, a SWOT analysis can create big problems. "When I became the leader at one business I ran," says Gary Cohen, "I inherited a few SWOT analyses that weren't worth the paper they were written on. Based on one of them, we had entered a new high-end merchandise category, and it was a mistake. The decision had been entirely based on the 'O'—opportunity, the chance to reach for this shiny star they wanted to go after. There was no linkage back to what we as a company were good or bad at. Nobody connected the dots. This category was growing, but the organization didn't have any particular strengths there. We weren't very good at dealing with the necessary distribution channels, and nobody ever figured out that we would have to build a specialized sales team from scratch. Beyond that, the downside of selling high-end merchandise if a market declined was never explored. When the economy did go south, we got killed."

What's Our Point of Difference? From SWOT to Strategic Competitive Advantage

At this time, let's look at our SWOT analysis so we can search for a "sweet spot of strengths," which we call our strategic competitive advantage, or SCA.

Our strategic competitive advantage is a superstrength, something we do better than anyone else. It's what truly distinguishes us from our peers or competitors. As Figure 3.6 illustrates, identifying the significant points of difference is the next step in TTW.

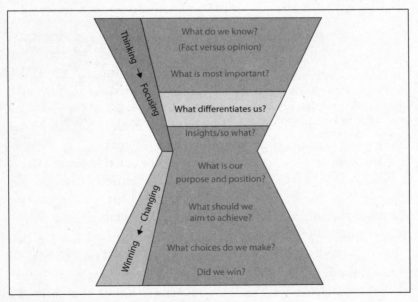

FIGURE 3.6. WHAT DIFFERENTIATES US?

Our SCA is why we can be secure that we will continue to be successful. Nolan Ryan was in the baseball business, and he remains one of the greatest pitchers of all time. Batters couldn't hit his pitches—he averaged more than one strikeout per inning over his career. His trademark was a blazing fastball, which was regularly clocked at over 100 miles per hour. This was his super-strength, his strategic competitive advantage, which he sustained year after year for much of his lengthy career.

Our SCAs separate us from the pack. Sometimes those SCAs are short-lived. But more durable competitive advantages, those lasting three years or more, are sustainable SCAs. And there are a number of factors that make a SCA sustainable:

- ► A breakthrough superior product that cannot easily be duplicated, especially one protected by trademark or patent (Botox, Gatorade, *Star Wars*, Angry Birds).
- ► A superior supply chain cost position (cornering the hazelnut market, if you're Nutella).
- ► Specialized know-how (oil spill cleanup, Hubbell telescope repair).
- ► Strong brand equity (Coca-Cola, Chanel, Tiffany, the New York Yankees).

When Toyota pioneered hybrid vehicles with the innovative Prius, it had almost the entire market for several years. Until other carmakers were able to respond, Toyota had a sustainable strategic competitive advantage. Mickey Mouse is a beloved worldwide icon and has been a sustainable SCA for the Walt Disney Company since the 1930s. Looked at in this light, Nolan Ryan was a sustainable SCA for whatever team he played on. He was one of a kind with a superior product that would never be duplicated. His major league career spanned 27 years, and the speed of his fastball was undiminished for more than two decades. Because sustainable SCAs are so valuable—and rare—they are worth pursuing.

Identifying an SCA means taking an in-depth look at our positives and negatives. Here's an example. All Clean is a company that manufactures a line of antibacterial hand wipes. When it conducted its SWOT analysis, its strengths were strong brand name recognition, a reputation for making a quality product, and a loyal base of repeat customers. Weaknesses included shelving inconsistencies—not being stocked in the aisle where most consumers expected to find its products—and the perception that the products were more expensive and less convenient than competing liquid hand sanitizers.

Opportunities for All Clean included a growing consumer focus on health and wellness, specifically a heightened awareness of the importance of clean hands; an increasingly mobile society, with its demands for convenient, on-the-go products; and several winters with virulent, widespread flu outbreaks. It's worth underscoring for all businesses that opportunity can reside in "bad news." (For example, Duracell sells more batteries with a hurricane looming, and companies specializing in roofing, construction, and carpet cleaning also view storms as destructive events that create more business.) External threats identified by All Clean included aggressive competition from other brands and private labels, and well-publicized statements from healthcare professionals, promoting soap and water, not hand wipes, as the "gold standard" for cleanliness. (See Table 3.2.)

TABLE 3.2.   ALL CLEAN HAND WIPES

Internal	External
Strengths	*Opportunities*
▶ Strong brand recognition ▶ All Clean branded product outperforms other players on key attributes ▶ Loyal consumer base— number one brand in private households ▶ Number one brand in hand wipes, segment leader for 30+ years	▶ Growing consumer trend of health and wellness—germ consciousness and heightened awareness of hand cleaning/sanitizing needs ▶ New flu strains and other viruses may extend flu season ▶ Growing investment in new hand hygiene technologies by independent third parties ▶ Consumers busy lifestyles continue to drive need for more convenient/ on-the-go products
Weaknesses	*Threats*
▶ Lack of unique brand positioning ▶ Production plant running below capacity ▶ Not shelved where consumers expect to find us ▶ Packaging not as convenient as liquid hand sanitizers ▶ Cost per use perceived as greater than hand sanitizers	▶ Other wipes manufacturers are investing heavily in research and development (R&D) ▶ Other hand sanitizers have stronger germ kill equity ▶ Competitors have broader distribution ▶ More healthcare professionals are saying that soap and water is the gold standard

How did All Clean look at its SWOT analysis to find its sustainable strategic competitive advantage? By connecting the dots. It coupled its number one internal strength with its number one external opportunity, and linked its strong, positive brand identification with the emerging trend in consumer awareness of health and wellness issues. (See Figure 3.7.)

Use the list of <u>s</u>trengths in the context of <u>o</u>pportunities to identify strategic <u>c</u>ompetitive <u>a</u>dvantages.	
Internal	**External**
Strengths	**Opportunities**
• Strong household brand associated with high quality	• Growing consumer trend of health and wellness
• Loyal consumer base • Best-in-class manufacturing facilities	• Consolidation of smaller customers, which simplifies sales and distribution

(Positives)

FIGURE 3.7.   FROM SWOT TO SCA
Source: GlobalEdg LLC. All Rights Reserved.

As the senior managers at Jamba Juice sought to identify its SCA, they reviewed the strengths that still defined the company despite the tough times it had experienced. It had innovation skills that virtually ensured a flow of new products. It had scale within the very fragmented smoothie and juice category that was characterized by mom-and-pop stores and small local chains. Its individual stores had sales volumes that were twice as large as its nearest competitor. Its base of consumers in California, the biggest smoothie and juice market in the country, was large and growing, giving it a dominant market share. The supply chain that provided Jamba with the necessary goods (everything from fresh fruits to napkins and straws) and services was solid.

The company culture, deeply grounded in the belief that Jamba's mission was to inspire and simplify healthy living, was very strong. Jamba's products were superior to its peers' in their taste, quality, and wellness benefits. And their portability was a perfect fit for an active on-the-go lifestyle. Importantly, the

Jamba Juice brand was iconic. Awareness of the brand extended far beyond its actual size and even its geographic distribution. And mere mention of the Jamba Juice name brought a smile and warm feelings both to ardent fans and even light users.

So there were many strengths from which Jamba identified the top five as: scale in the segment; company culture; product taste and quality; wellness benefits; and portability. These five were viewed as sources for Jamba's competitive advantage. And when Jamba looked for a *sustainable* competitive advantage, all agreed it was the Jamba Juice brand—a powerful equity that should be enduring and provide a platform for growth for many years to come.

Chapter Summary

► TTW harnesses the power of asking the right questions in the right order. The *hourglass* is the structure that guides us through the process.

► Clearly defining the umbrella statement to frame the scope, provide direction, and secure alignment on our issue goes a long way toward determining our success in addressing it.

► The step-by-step process of TTW leads us through convergent thinking to use the seven Cs framework and SWOT analysis to compile our data and fact base and identify our strategic competitive advantage.

EMMA CREATES HER SWOT ANALYSIS

Emma is concerned that the large number of new graduates in her chosen field represents a threat to her job search. She knows it is important to pinpoint her competitive advantage—the leg up she has on other applicants. *Her skill at technical writing, experience in HR, coupled with her fluency in Arabic and her level of comfort in dealing with other languages and cultures, meshes well with the rise of companies having employees and business interests around the globe.* Emma realizes these skills are her competitive advantage and make her uniquely qualified. They are enduring assets that few other applicants are likely to have, even those with more work experience. Emma's SWOT is outlined in Table 3.3.

TABLE 3.3. EMMA'S SWOT

Internal	External
Strengths	*Opportunities*
What do I do well? ▶ Technical writing—strong understanding of data, how to tell a story with facts ▶ Fluency in Arabic/overseas life experience ▶ Measure development, measure change ▶ Knowledge of "best practices" in corporate, healthcare, and private business units ▶ Strong interpersonal skills—harvesting/ sustaining relationships	*What external trends or conditions can I or the competition capitalize on?* ▶ Companies with global business interests and global HR needs ▶ Networking through professional and personal connections ▶ Fast-moving environment ▶ Shift in "big data" focus from larger organizations ▶ People-driven industry and cultural shift
Weaknesses	*Threats*
What do I do poorly? ▶ Shyness/reticence, soft speaking voice ▶ Risk averse—fear of making a huge mistake ▶ People pleaser—always trying to make *everybody* happy	*What external trends or conditions should I be wary of?* ▶ Many recent college graduates in my field ▶ Applicant overload at entry level and next level up— where I am

By answering the questions what do we know?, what is important?, and what differentiates us? we are halfway through the top of the hourglass. This knowledge is powerful, but we still have to know what to do with it. In Chapter 4, we look more closely at how we use our findings to formulate *conclusions* and examine *strategies*.

Chapter 3 Exercises

Here are some questions and exercises to guide you in applying the TTW principles. As you spend time with each of the principles, your overall competence in thinking strategically will improve. So spend the time, and the results will follow.

What Are We Trying to Solve?

Mastering a TTW Umbrella Statement

The umbrella statement lies at the heart of the Think to Win process. "What, *exactly,* are we trying to solve?" The first and most important step in the TTW methodology is identifying the big issue. By identifying where the problem begins, the correct place for analysis is pinpointed and you can now begin to address the challenge! Consider the following questions:

- ▶ What are you trying to solve? *Must* be answered.
- ▶ Who can help me best define it?
- ▶ What am I trying to change?

Exercise: Creating an Umbrella Statement
(Can be done at individual or group level)

1. Individually consider the question: "What am I really trying to solve?"
2. Capture in one to two sentences.
3. Review with the following criteria in mind:
   - Is it clear and succinct?
   - Is it focused?
   - Is it free of solutions?
   - Is there tension and a sense of urgency (what is at risk)?
4. Have a conversation with other stakeholders to clarify issues and gain alignment.
5. Output: an umbrella statement that will set the stage for your analysis.

What Do We Know?

When we complete our umbrella statement, we start to identify and process what we know about our issue or problem. We want our fact base and data gathering to be robust but not overwhelming.

Mastering the Use of TTW Frameworks

Employ the use of TTW frameworks to identify and capture critical data. TTW frameworks are great tools that can guide you through the process of capturing and sorting your information.

The Seven C Framework

Utilize a seven C framework to "bucket data" for focused analysis. List the data most related to the issue. *Collect only the facts that are most relevant!* Ask, *Why is that important for us to know?*

For internal analysis ask: *What do we know? What is going on inside the company?*

- ► **Company.** Everything going on within the company, except people. This would include financials, structure, history, products, brand, vision, systems, mission, and values. All these data go under company.
- ► **Colleagues.** Everything that relates to people: employee morale, engagement, capabilities, competencies, skills; anything that would normally be examined under "people." (It is often called "people;" it's modified here to fit the seven C terminology.)

For external analysis ask: *What do we know? What is going on in the external marketplace?*

- ► **Category.** Where do you and your competitors "do battle in the marketplace"? You may be in several categories, depending on the company and products.
- ► **Customers and consumers.** These could be one and the same or completely different.
- ► **Competitors.** Whomever you are "doing battle with" or competing against within the category.
- ► **Community.** Think of the word **STEEP**—*Social trends* (see the mnemonic that follows); what trends are happening in society, in the environment in which you live?. How is *technology* advancing? Is the macro *economic* climate changing? Are *environmental* concerns heightening? Is the *political and regulatory* climate becoming more or less favorable?

STEEP

S = Social trends
T = Technology
E = Economic
E = Environment
P = Politics/Regulations

Exercise: Populating a Framework
(Can be done at individual or group level.)

1. Use the seven C situational assessment framework to capture relevant internal and external information.
2. Support your findings with relevant facts.
3. Ask whether this information links to the umbrella statement.
4. Make sure all the "Cs" are represented with relevant data.
5. Have a conversation with other stakeholders to clarify and gain alignment.
6. Output is a seven C analysis that will set the stage for determining strengths, weaknesses, opportunities, and threats.

The deliverable is a completed section of framework to inform your SWOT analysis.

What Is Most Important?

We need to carefully examine the information we have to determine what is most important. The TTW approach to a SWOT analysis provides us with a valuable tool.

Mastering the SWOT Tool to Drive TTW Thinking

For internal strengths and weaknesses, ask the questions: What do we do really well? What don't we do really well? When answering the questions, remember to see through the lens of the competition! Is it a real strength?

For external opportunities and threats, consider the following:

▶ These are trends in the marketplace; the marketplace is moving at warp speed, making it harder to foresee the future.
▶ At this point, an opportunity is an opportunity for both your organization and the competitor; it is not yet an action. It is a trend.

Set the information up in a four-quadrant matrix that aligns positive factors, both internal and external, and negative factors, both internal and external, with one another, as shown in Figure 3.8.

	Internal	External
	Strengths	**Opportunities**
Positives	What do we do well?	What external trends or conditions can we or the competition capitalize on?
	Weaknesses	**Threats**
Negatives	What can we improve?	What external trends or conditions should we be wary of?

FIGURE 3.8.   A SWOT TOOL.

Exercise: Creating a SWOT Matrix

This exercise can be done at individual or group level.

1. Gather your framework (seven Cs).
2. Create four charts—one for each letter of SWOT.
3. Use the internal Cs to determine strengths and weaknesses.
4. Use the external Cs to determine opportunities and threats.
5. Use Figure 3.8 to capture your information.
6. Have a conversation with other stakeholders to clarify and gain alignment.

The deliverable is a completed draft of a SWOT analysis.

What Differentiates Us?

Understanding our significant points of difference helps us develop a list of our sustainable advantages.

Mastering How to Identify a Strategic Competitive Advantage

Ask yourself the following:

- ► What is the source of our competitive advantage?
- ► Does this separate us from the competition?
- ► Does it really provide us with leverage and margin in the marketplace?
- ► Using the SWOT analysis, focus on the strengths:
  - ● What is the source of our competitive advantage? What makes our organization unique?
  - ● What is our sustainable competitive advantage? How long can we hold it? *Three years is the rule of thumb.*

Ask thought provoking questions such as: What is Toyota's competitive advantage? Apple's? Our competitors'? Who are the competitors we might not be thinking about?

Exercise: SCA

This exercise can be done at an individual or group level.

1. Use the strength section of the SWOT analysis. Determine the SCA for your organization.
2. Answer the following questions:
   - ● What really differentiates us?
   - ● Is it a source or sustainable?
   - ● If it exists, how do we retain it?
   - ● If it does not exist, what do we need to be thinking about to create one?
3. Have a conversation with other stakeholders to clarify and gain alignment.

The deliverable is that the SCA is identified and aligned.

Organizational Assessment

Use the following table as a checklist for identifying TTW principles and practices. This will help you to better understand where your organization needs to focus your energies. To get an idea where you believe your organization stands, read through each statement and jot down a rating from 1 to 5:

Concept/Process	Scale: 1= Low, 5 = High
We are able to clearly and consistently define our most significant business issues in one to two sentences.	
We leverage our internal strengths when making decisions about our organization's strategies.	
Our organization's core strategies are based on a careful review of our strengths, weaknesses, opportunities, and challenges.	
We use a common set of tools for data collection and organization.	
We are able to articulate our competitive advantage(s) in the marketplace.	

Review individual items. Look for items where your organization scored lower (3 and below) and think about the following questions:

► What do I believe is driving the score?
► What do I need to stop, start, or continue doing?
► What do I want the result to be?

Key To Winning

When Vice Chairman Ed Shirley took over Procter & Gamble's (P&G) vast global grooming and beauty group, the umbrella statement he agreed on with his senior managers was very straightforward: Jumpstart the group's stagnant performance by identifying ways to accelerate growth in rapidly expanding developing markets where results had been very inconsistent.

Even a quick look at the group's sales showed a patchwork quilt of penetration: very little in Latin America and Central and Eastern Europe; very strong in China, but almost none in India and Southeast Asia. Ed could see that P&G was overlooking great opportunities in some of the fastest growing regions of the world. But Ed also learned that several past initiatives to pick up the pace in developing countries had resulted in costly failures—several P&G brands just couldn't gain traction and make money in what had appeared to be fertile markets for growth. So what were the key issues? What was standing in P&G's way, and what could Ed and his team do differently? Ed was hoping that a TTW-like process would point the way.

Keeping the Blenders Whirring

When James D. White arrived as the new CEO of Jamba Juice in December 2008, the iconic smoothies and juice company had racked up losses for the year of $149 million. To James, the first day on the job felt like he'd been strapped into an amusement park ride, the Tower of Terror, where "the bottom disappears beneath you and you drop into freefall." He knew there were a lot of data and facts to sort through. And he also knew strong emotions and beliefs had to be heard but filtered. And he and his team had very little time to identify key issues, assess the implications, and develop an action plan to present to a very edgy and apprehensive board of directors. If the TTW process didn't deliver, Jamba's famed in-store blenders wouldn't be whirring much longer.

As we saw in Chapter 3, the initial steps in TTW start with a large amount of facts and data that define what we know—what's our situation? Then by using our umbrella statement to help determine what's important, we start our convergent thinking process that filters out peripheral or irrelevant data. If we are working on an issue with a group or team, this will be a very iterative process—lots of discussion and dialogue. (How important is competitor Smoothie King's growth rate? Or the number of Jamba smoothie flavors that failed? Or how many P&G deodorant brands are available in global markets?) All this discussion gives us great alignment.

With the right umbrella statement—one that's clear, concise, and focused and that captures the urgency of the issue—and with our five principles for guidance—the identification of what's important points us toward fact-based findings. These are some nonjudgmental observations that are supported by the important data. (Jamba stores in strip malls do better than stand-alone units. Franchised Jamba stores have higher profits than company-owned stores. P&G shampoos succeed more often in Southeast Asia than in Latin America.)

These findings represent chunks of data that can help frame the next phase of TTW—seeking insights and then conclusions, or a statement of key issues.

As Figure 4.1 illustrates, finding insights and conclusions is the final phase of thinking and focusing in the TTW process.

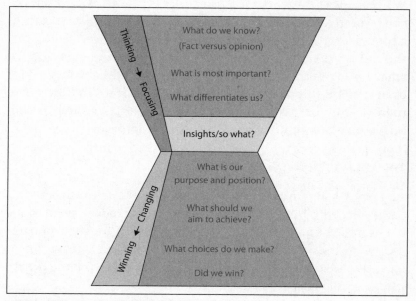

FIGURE 4.1.   SEEKING INSIGHTS.

Here's the way Ed Shirley describes it. As he looked at the findings from the situation assessment for the grooming and beauty group, he noticed that all of P&G's developing country initiatives were taken by individual brands and product categories—shampoo went to India; deodorant went to Mexico; cosmetics to the Philippines; body wash to Argentina. None of the efforts was coordinated either by P&G at the country level or by brands across product categories.

"Brazil is one of the largest deodorant markets in the world," Ed says. "When our deodorant team went in there alone and built a plan to grow our market share, our big well-established competitor there, Unilever, shifted money from one of their other categories and squashed our deodorant team like a bug. And 12 to 18 months later, they came home with their tails between their legs."

The findings showed Ed and his team that this uncoordinated approach was often repeated, always with the same result. As they puzzled over these outcomes, the insight came: P&G wasn't leveraging a key competitive strength and advantage—the company's considerable scale.

"One of my fundamental principles is that the whole should always be greater than the sum of its parts. And we were acting as a sum of the parts company," says Ed.

And with this insight, one of Ed's key issues emerged: In what countries and with what brands could P&G bring its scale to bear to bolster its odds for success. As we'll see in Chapter 5, moving from key issues to governing statements, strategies, and action plans also takes a very disciplined approach.

Facing a Critical Juncture

At Jamba, soon after James White arrived, he scheduled an off-site retreat with his top dozen executives to introduce them to the TTW process and come up with a rescue plan for the company. This would be an action learning event—the Jamba management team would learn TTW by applying it real time to Jamba's very pressing problems.

As the starting point for answering the What do we know? question at the top of the hourglass, the team was given "prework" to complete before the retreat began. In addition to gathering facts and data about their functions and areas of responsibility, they were asked to identify recent changes they had observed, both inside and outside the company, additional changes they anticipated in the near future, and the challenges or opportunities those changes represented.

At the retreat, agreeing and aligning on their umbrella statement turned out to be quick: *We are at a critical juncture in the life of this company. If we do not stabilize our financial condition and enhance our revenue, the business will fail.*

Team members discussed and evaluated the facts, data, and prework, making their way through the second question, What is most important? Surprisingly, especially to James, this analysis was something that had not been done previously. "I don't think the prior management had a real understanding of Jamba's strengths and weaknesses, our marketplace opportunities and threats," says James. After the SWOT assessment was completed, the team focused on key issues and agreed on five:

1. **Business model: company-owned versus franchise.** Jamba's focus on company-owned stores was adversely impacting its balance sheet. Many company-owned stores were underperforming, raising several subissues: Should Jamba close them, even if they were new? Did Jamba need a new business model that focused on franchised rather than company-owned stores? If so, how would Jamba ensure the quality of the Jamba brand?

2. **Cash/liquidity.** Jamba had negative cash flow. Costs were already cut by 15 percent, but it wasn't enough. Jamba needed to find additional savings in stores without compromising quality or the customer experience. Jamba also needed to find cost-cutting opportunities at headquarters without jeopardizing its ability to function or damaging employee morale.

3. **Right-sizing.** Prior management had an oversized vision of Jamba as the "Starbucks of smoothies." It foresaw a potential for 10,000 stores nationwide. But with the Great Recession in full swing, a more realistic, fact-based assessment suggested just over a quarter of that number—somewhere around 2,500. Could Jamba thrive with a smaller footprint? Were there other formats that would expand growth prospects?

4. **Smoothies or smoothies plus?** Should Jamba focus on smoothies, its core business, or should it offer a wider menu— breakfast, lunch, and dinner options, and warm beverages, especially in winter months?

5. **Licensing.** With the strong Jamba brand, the company had an opportunity to establish licensing agreements that would place Jamba products in grocery and convenience stores across the country. Could Jamba do this while maintaining high standards and without adversely affecting franchisees?

It was a very productive retreat for James and the Jamba team. As we'll see in Chapter 5, it set the stage for a multiyear turn-around action plan.

Insights from Careful Analysis— Not Always A Falling Apple

It's worth looking at the role of insights in formulating key issues and in helping to set a direction for the rest of the TTW process. Often when we think of insights, we imagine an Isaac Newton type of event. From a falling apple hitting someone on the head comes the discovery of gravity. While insights can strike suddenly, usually they come from careful analysis of data and understanding of the dynamics that frame a specific issue.

In marketing, for instance, insights shed light on *why* people behave the way they do and what choices they make. They tap into an underlying need, or desire, or belief, or value system. They usually are simple, but nonetheless, profound.

Professor Theodore Levitt, the Harvard Business School guru, gives a great example: People don't want quarter-inch drills. They want quarter-inch holes.

An insight is that *Aha!* moment, the revelation of an undiscovered truth that often was "hiding in plain sight." Once you see it, you can't "unsee" it, nor can you imagine why it hadn't occurred to you before. Insights lead us to discover new ways to think about our issues and businesses.

For example, it was a simple but profound insight that enabled Oscar Mayer, the hot dog and cold cuts giant, to tap into a fast growing area of the otherwise stagnant processed meat market.

The company was trying to figure out how to make bologna more appealing to mothers so they would pack more bologna sandwiches into their children's lunchboxes, when they realized it wasn't that mothers didn't like bologna. These time-challenged mothers of children in elementary schools really disliked fixing lunches. It was one more thing they had to do in the morning when they were already too busy. And their kids weren't too thrilled with what they prepared, which was another disincentive. Kids found mom's lunches boringly repetitive and short on creativity.

And it was from that insight that the convenient, appealing time-saving Lunchables brand was born. With literally hundreds of varieties and permutations, the brand has grown into a very profitable billion-dollar bonanza for Oscar Mayer, now going on more than 20 years.

For Keurig, the insight was understanding how many people wanted to make a single cup of good coffee, conveniently and quickly. These habitual coffee drinkers were generally dissatisfied with other alternatives. They considered granulated instant coffee, or coffee purchased from vending machines, to be of inferior quality. Other good coffee options such as going out to a specialty shop like Starbucks, were too expensive and often inaccessible during the workday or late at night. By offering consumers a wide range of high-quality coffees and other hot and cold drinks, ready in less than a minute, with no prep or clean up, at prices averaging about 50 cents per cup, Keurig has become the global leader in single-cup brewed beverages.

Daryl Brewster, CEO of CECP (formerly the Committee Encouraging Corporate Philanthropy), describes an insight at a critical moment for Kraft's food business in Mexico that not only prevented a sales loss of $70 million in that country, but also resulted in the creation of what is now more than a half-billion dollar business in the United States.

At the time, Daryl was head in the United States and Canada of Kraft's $6 billion snack, confection, cereal, beverage, and pet food portfolio, which included such power brands as Oreo and Chips Ahoy! cookies; LifeSavers candy; Post cereals; and Tang and Crystal Light beverages. Just two weeks after Daryl assumed added responsibility for Kraft's Mexican business, the government imposed a tax that more than doubled the cost of fructose—the key ingredient in their most profitable products— Tang, Kool-Aid, and Crystal Light. A quick estimate put the likely hit at $100 million.

As a long-time believer in TTW, Daryl knew the importance of putting together a solid situation assessment that would inform their strategies and actions. Absent the assessment, the leadership team assumed that price increases, lobbying the government for a change, and asking for budget relief from Kraft headquarters were the only real options.

The situation assessment and findings wound up showing otherwise. Due to their popularity with less affluent Mexican consumers, the beverage impact would be significant, but likely closer to about $70 million as repriced products became less affordable.

And as Daryl and the team looked at the situation assessment, *affordability* was glaringly critical. The team immediately decided on strategies to lower costs across the board with a focus on reducing cost of goods by reformulating from fructose to sugar and on initiating lobbying activities with the government.

But more was needed, which is when the insight hit. In addition to making the beverages available in their normal pack sizes in jars and pouches, they would pack them in single-serve sachets, something not tried in Mexico or in any other market in Kraft's global operations. The insight was masterful on many levels. The lower price of single-serves would make them affordable to almost all consumers except the very lowest economic group. Its format would make single-serves convenient to use with bottled water that's popular in Mexico due to tainted water issues. The sachets small size (12 flavors of single-serves could be racked on an 8-by-12-inch rack) meant they would gain increased acceptance in the cramped food stalls (tiendas) so popular in Mexico. And even powerful competitors like Coke and Pepsi would view single-serves as complementary to their bottled water businesses.

The product was a great hit in Mexico and within a year, Crystal Light single-serves were introduced in the United States where within three years it was a $300 million business. Daryl went on to use TTW throughout his entire portfolio and led his business to record top and bottom line growth. He followed his success at Kraft by taking over the troubled Krispy Kreme Doughnuts company where he reversed financial declines, reduced debt, and expanded operations globally.

Actionable Insights Lead to Key Issues

Of course, all insights must be actionable for them to be worthwhile. They must assist us in forming our key issues, or conclusions, that address our umbrella statements. It's coming up with solid key issues that enable us to move forward with the TTW process.

And we know our key issues are solid if they tie together the most important findings and persuasively define a major problem or diagnose a significant issue. They also should point to a course of action that addresses threats and weaknesses as well as opportunities and strengths.

It's also important that we stay focused on the vital few—seven to ten key issues may make us feel like we're covering all contingencies. But research and experience show that seven to ten are far too many. Here is where we employ the 90-10 rule to pare down our key issues to a more effective maximum of *four to six*.

So What? Implications: What to Do and Why

Armed with key issues and conclusions, the next step is to drive for implications. Our implications move us toward the action phase of TTW. They explain what we should do and why in a way that's clear and actionable. Plus they are memorable and motivating, capturing insights that will significantly affect our issues. Let's look at just a couple of examples:

> **Key issue.** Our largest competitor has purchased low-cost production capability and is driving down prices in the category.
> **Implication.** A timely upgrade of our production capability isn't possible, so we have to cut our input and labor costs in order to remain competitive.
>
> **Key issue.** Farmers' markets are the most rapidly growing sector in food retailing.
> **Implication.** Unless we build a distribution infrastructure, we can't serve farmers' markets and we miss out on great sales growth.

Implications are the bridge to the start of the action phase—the forming of visions, governing statements, and goals that we take up in Chapter 5.

KEY ISSUES AND IMPLICATIONS—NURTURING NUTRITION NATION

This SWOT matrix for the Nutrition Nation chain of health and nutrition retail stores clearly identifies changing market dynamics, including the growing competition of online shopping for supplements. Careful study of this SWOT matrix led to the identification of a vital few key issues and implications, which became the basis for developing a vision and goals.

(Continues)

Nutrition Nation: Integrating Marketing SWOT

Strengths	Opportunities
▶ High gross margin % ▶ Engaged loyalists driving business ▶ Associates turnover lower than industry average ▶ Robust customer database representing 90 percent of sales ▶ Results of new store design and rebranded stores showing positive movement ▶ Motivated, highly engaged workforce ▶ Run for cause—charity reputation ▶ New technology for on-site customer service	▶ Consumer preferences moving to natural/organic products ▶ Consumer price perception that large retailers are lower ▶ 60 percent of consumers are preshopping online for pricing/information ▶ 30 percent of all customers drive 70 percent of volume ▶ Aging baby boomer population increasing our pool of customers ▶ Store/generic brands increasingly seen as same quality as national brands
Weaknesses	**Threats**
▶ Low brand awareness ▶ Out of stock issues ▶ Dated technology ▶ Outdated store look (average store 12 years old) ▶ Store base scattered geographically ▶ Product packaging does not currently align with new branding ▶ Product not differentiated enough	▶ Increasing availability of supplements online ▶ Increasing government regulations on what we can say to customers ▶ Competitors—opening stores more quickly than us in key cities ▶ 40 percent of our customers are buying at least a few of their supplements through mass retailers. Many mass stores focusing on category ▶ Non-top-tier mall traffic decreasing while occupancy costs are increasing ▶ Perception of category is confusing—products not differentiated; benefits and quality levels are unclear ▶ Competitors going after mall customers

KEY ISSUES AND IMPLICATIONS

Key Issue 1—Low Brand Awareness

We suffer from low overall brand awareness. Even those consumers who are aware of the brand do not have opinions on key attributes, such as product mix, service, pricing, and so on.

Implications

Low awareness is a limiting factor in acquiring new customers, which impacts our ability to compete effectively. In addition, understanding consumer price perceptions will help us execute a pricing strategy that allows us to effectively compete. We must have new brand positioning and execute quickly.

Key Issue 2—Increased Competition from Other Channels

With 40 percent of our customers shopping for at least some of their supplements at larger mass retailers as well as online because of price and convenience, we are facing increased competition from other channels.

Implications

Effective communication and execution of new training with our store associates will be necessary to clearly articulate reasons for buying from us rather than from mass stores and online.

Providing a customer experience that cannot be duplicated in other channels is critical. Continuously developing associate knowledge and customer engagement skills as well as identifying, testing and implementing in-store events such as health screenings, sampling programs, and partnership with vendors will help create a differentiated experience.

Key Issue 3—Regulations Limit What We Can Say

There are legal constraints on what we can say and the claims we can make about our products. We tend to take a conservative

(Continues)

stance when interpreting regulations, while competitors will often take a more liberal interpretation or make unsubstantiated claims.

Implications

A driver of shopping at specialty stores and online is to acquire information. We become less competitive when we can't provide the sought-after information. Accelerating our efforts to engage our legal department to develop a more comprehensive communications strategy will help us more strongly communicate benefits while maintaining regulatory compliance. In addition, a concerted effort to challenge other companies' claims will help level the playing field.

Key Issue 4—Older Technology Is Limiting Execution of Online Channel Strategies

Aging technology is prohibiting us from servicing our customers at the same level that our competitors do. Today's consumers have higher expectations about shopping seamlessly across channels.

Implications

We are unable to effectively compete/service our customers, with our older technology platforms. New software is currently being tested in the United Kingdom prior to rolling out in the United States.

Key Issue 5—Declining Store Traffic

A reduction in store traffic can be partially attributed to the decline in mall traffic, which opens an opportunity for us to drive destination shopping through channel and marketing efforts.

Implications

Footsteps driven by malls are a significant source of our customer traffic. The activation of the new brand positioning will have a positive impact by driving mall customers into our stores, thus increasing store traffic. Continued efforts to improve conversion through associate training will help ensure that those shoppers who walk into the store make a purchase.

The step-by-step approach for moving from umbrella statements to key issues and conclusions and implications is detailed in the Key Issues exercises at the end of this chapter.

EMMA'S KEY ISSUES AND IMPLICATIONS

Having looked at her position vis-a-vis other applicants, and in the context of today's HR career demands, Emma comes to several important conclusions. She understands she is at a critical but highly flexible point in her career from which she'd be able to grow and explore opportunities in any number of directions. The implication she draws from those options and opportunities is that she has few limitations to her possibilities—many fewer than she originally thought. Because of her strong understanding of corporate and healthcare needs, she draws the implication that she would be able to apply this knowledge in a wide range of possible industries, or even in government or nonprofit institutions. Her young, moldable skill set includes capabilities that are very much in demand—in particular, fluency in Arabic and her technical writing skills.

Chapter Summary

- ▶ Looking at the top half of the hourglass, there is a clear line of connection from the initial What Do We Know step to the transition point of So What, the implications for action. The line links data and facts to our findings, which in turn lead to key issues and ultimately to our implications.
- ▶ Insights are important for revealing undiscovered truths that often are hiding in plain sight. Once we see the truth, we can't "unsee" it. With insights, we discover new ways to think about our issues.
- ▶ Key issues, or conclusions, tie related findings together, establishing those that are most important and pointing to a course of action.
- ▶ Implications flow directly from key issues. They explain what to do and why. They are clear and actionable and also must be memorable and motivating.

Chapter 4 Exercises

Insights and Implications

What insights have we gained and what are their implications?

Mastering Key Issues

Begin by asking:

- ▶ What did I learn from my analysis?
- ▶ Can I clearly communicate the information in a way that others will understand? How should I best articulate this?
- ▶ Am I missing anything? People? The organization? The marketplace? The community?
- ▶ Which are most important? Rank the top five in order of importance based on relevance, ability to act on, criticality, and urgency.

Exercise: Key Issues

This exercise can be done at the individual or group level.

1. Review the information collected in the situation assessment (seven Cs framework, SWOT, and SCA) and identify the key issues.
2. Think about the following:
   - ● What conclusions can I draw?
   - ● What high-level actions do I need to consider?
3. For each key issue, create a corresponding implication statement.
4. Combine risk and action in your statement.
5. Review your statement to assure clarity and achieve alignment.

The deliverable is a draft of key issues and implications.

Exercise: Key Issues
(Recommended for larger group or team)

Create a *wall of issues* by asking everyone to individually reflect on the situation assessment, up to and including the SWOT/ SCA. Ask each participant to consider what he or she has learned from the situation assessment. Ask all participants to identify what they believe the key issues to be and write them all down on sticky notes, one issue per note.

After the participants are finished, ask them to bring their collection of notes to the front of the room and place them on flip chart paper (see Figure 4.2). You will have a lot of sticky notes. Ask the group to read through all identified issues for clarification and then remove duplicates.

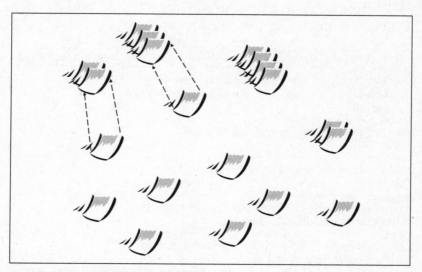

FIGURE 4.2. WALL OF ISSUES.

Sort issues into categories by working with the group to identify common themes among those that remain. At the end of the process, you will probably have about five to seven categories that when labeled and summarized will be used to draft key issue statements (see Figure 4.3).

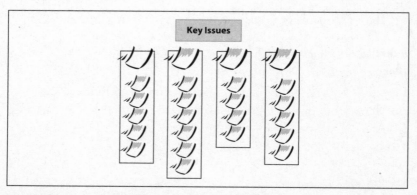

FIGURE 4.3. SORTED WALL OF KEY ISSUES.

Organizational Assessment

Use the following table as a checklist for identifying TTW principles and practices. This will help you to better understand where you and your team need to focus your energies. To get an idea where you believe your organization stands, read through each statement and jot down a rating:

Concept/Process	Scale: 1 = Low, 5 = High
We thoroughly understand the issues we need to address before we make decisions on goals/strategies and plans.	
We identify critical issues and prioritize them effectively.	
We know how to streamline from many to a few key issues.	
We prioritize our efforts on the appropriate business issues that will create clear direction.	
We know where to direct our efforts when we begin talking about important issues.	

When you have completed the checklist and scoring, review the individual items. Look for those items on which you have scored 3 and below, and think about the following:

▶ What do I believe is driving the score?
▶ What do I need to stop, start, or continue doing?
▶ What do I hope the result will be?

CHAPTER 5

Vision: Seeing the Future of Winning

---

*"If you don't know where you're going,
you'll end up someplace else."*

—YOGI BERRA

This is one of our favorite Yogi Berra quotes. Like many of his unintentionally humorous sayings, it reveals a deeper truth, in this case about the importance of having a sense of purpose. In TTW, that sense of purpose is found in what we call a *vision* or *governing statement*. It serves the same purpose as highway guardrails that keep us on the straight and narrow.

Developing a vision marks the first phase in the bottom of the hourglass and begins the transition from convergent to divergent thinking. Similar to the top of the hourglass, crafting a successful vision depends on asking the right question, which is: How do we position ourselves for success?

While the situation assessment in the upper part of the hour-glass provides a panoramic view of the present, the vision gives a view of the desired future—what success will look like. It helps clarify what we intend to do in order to move forward.

Simple, Concise, Clear, and Compelling

It was a simple but precise vision that guided Keurig as it expanded from solely selling single-serving coffeepots and coffee-makers to businesses to entering the home market with a range of brewing systems and beverages. Keurig's vision: *A brewer on every countertop, a beverage for every occasion.*

"The clearer the statement is, the simpler it is, the more com-pelling it is, and the more memorable and more inspiring it will be," says Keurig Green Mountain board of directors' member Dave Moran. "One of the key things that has driven our success is the tremendous clarity around our vision of how we would approach growth. We boiled it down to one sentence that every-body could remember. And then made sure it was understood by all. Everyone here, regardless of their function or level in the company, knows that sentence, and knows that is exactly what we are trying to achieve. The statement was really descriptive of how we intended to grow the business."

To be effective, a vision must be unique, memorable, and free of jargon. And it should point the way forward to specific strategies, initiatives, and plans. Importantly, to be best of class, vision must tie closely to our SWOT and SCA from the top of the hourglass, being very actionable and realizable, utilizing our strengths and opportunities and acknowledging our threats and weaknesses.

At the other end of the spectrum are visions that may be very aspirational and even inspirational in their rhetoric, but are totally disconnected both from the reality of the marketplace and the nexus of our SWOT and SCA. Soaring sentiments unre-lated to facts never translate into anything but trouble.

Let's see how formulating a vision can actually unify a com-pany and shape its values and culture. When WhiteWave Foods was established as a division of Dean Foods prior to its spinoff in 2012, it was an organization with no common processes, structures, or culture.

While part of Dean Foods, the various WhiteWave units operated very separately. "Horizon, the country's top selling organic milk, and Silk, the leading brand of soy milk, had been two Colorado start-ups," recalls Joe Scalzo, then WhiteWave president and chief operating officer, "and they were still being run like start-ups. We also had a coffee creamer business with two brands—International Delight and Land O'Lakes. They were three different businesses, with very different cultures and no one way of doing anything. There weren't even *three* ways of doing things. Whenever we launched a product, for example, the process was completely ad hoc. And on top of everything else, none of the units really liked the others. There was great disharmony."

Scalzo's first priority was to meld the three disparate pieces into a cohesive, cooperative whole. "We described the path the company had been on; then we asked everyone in the organization to help us answer the key questions: Who are we? What do we believe in? What do we believe about making money for our community? What do we believe about being profitable, and growing, and supporting sustainable agriculture? The answers that came back affirmed how deeply committed our people were to sustainability, to playing a positive role in the community, and to corporate responsibility. We then identified seven core values that became the linchpin to change and unify the company. Our vision statement of our purpose became *To be the Earth's favorite food company,* which pointed the direction for our growth."

Since WhiteWave went public, it has followed its "good earth" vision with great success as both profits and growth have risen to levels that are far superior to its former parent, Dean Foods. WhiteWave has come out strongly against genetically modified organism (GMO) foods, not just for its own products but for agriculture as a whole. It has switched to sustainable palm oil for its plant-based creamers. It also focuses on feeding the hungry, reducing its water use and greenhouse gas emissions, and increasing its use of recyclable packaging. Meanwhile, the market has rewarded the company for its ability to think strategically, its enthusiasm, its principles, and the consistency of its vision. WhiteWave became the fastest-growing food company in North America.

So visions really do matter. And so do governing statements, which is what we call a vision when it applies to part of a company—like a division or subsidiary—rather than the whole. It definitely mattered for Ed Shirley as he devised a governing statement for P&G's grooming and beauty group that would tie back to its umbrella statement, flow from a rigorous situation assessment, and guide its future growth activities in developing markets.

Ed's umbrella statement had identified the need to jump-start the group's stagnant performance by showing ways to accelerate growth in developing markets where results had been very inconsistent. Ed's governing statement gave definition to the ways.

Going into a developing market with just one product at a time diminished P&G's likelihood for significant penetration, impact, and success, and it failed to leverage P&G's product breadth.

"As we made our assessment, we thought about our prospective consumer, a woman getting ready to face her day. Stepping into the shower, she would use bar soap or body wash. She would wash her hair and maybe condition it; she would shave her legs. When she got out of the shower, she would put on body moisturizer, deodorant, facial moisturizer, cosmetics, maybe use a hair styling aid, and then she would finish with fragrance.

"Those are all things that a woman would do. Those are all products that we make; products we could sell her. But we weren't selling them all within the same markets. In some places she'd be able to buy body wash, but not deodorant, or vice versa. In other places she could buy hair products, but not razors or blades.

"The same was true of products for men. We were all over the body, just like we were all over the map. We were missing the chance to sell consumers a suite of products from P&G because we weren't looking at the daily regimen; we weren't looking at people holistically."

But going into more than a single developing market at a time with new product categories would diffuse P&G's efforts. So Ed's governing statement tied together all the elements: *Grooming and beauty products would drive accelerated growth for a range of product lines—for both her and him—in high growth, developing markets through coordinated action that would use P&Gs scale to make a difference.*

Ed and his team ultimately agreed on Brazil as their initial market. "Instead of going to Brazil as separate units," he says, "we went in as Procter & Gamble. We brought hair care, cosmetics, deodorants, skin care, body wash, wet shaving, and dry shaving. We brought everything to Brazil. Basically, it was an invasion and our competition was unable to defeat us piecemeal. They couldn't shift resources from one category to another, because we were everywhere.

"Our commercial team in Brazil was thrilled that it finally had one voice and one plan—one coordinated plan. When I came back to our headquarters in Cincinnati, I shared this with our P&G leadership team. Our CEO thought it was a big idea, so he asked the laundry & household care group to do the same thing, followed by the health & well-being group. And wouldn't you know, all of P&G went to Brazil.

"Now, for the first time, we played a company game, and we leveraged our competitive scale. And our first-year results were 30 percent growth."

Governing Statements—Restraining but Not Restrictive

At times, a governing statement of purpose and position (see Figure 5.1) can, and should, serve to restrain actions. That was the case with Braun, the global leader in electric shavers.

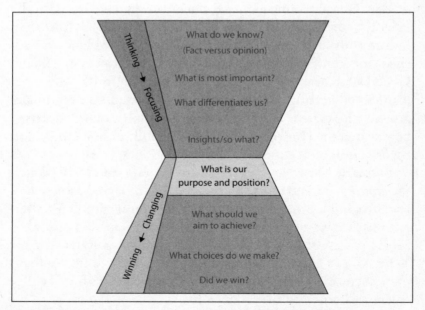

FIGURE 5.1. WHAT IS OUR PURPOSE AND POSITION?

Although Gillette acquired Braun for its razor business and shaving expertise, Braun also used its electric small motor skills to produce a vast array of appliances and gadgets from food processors and meat grinders to alarm clocks and wristwatches that it tried to market around the world with poor results year after year. In fact, Braun hadn't made a targeted budget for close to a decade.

So the governing statement developed by and for Braun was straightforward: *Braun would focus on dry shaving and ensure that each product line would minimally return greater than its cost capital.* It was fine for Braun to sell meat grinders in Russia, but only if it would cover its costs and then some.

Yet governing statements also can be, or can become, too restrictive and narrow as market dynamics change, opportunities emerge, and threats become clearer. WhiteWave Foods provides an excellent illustration. When WhiteWave formulated its 2007 governing statement, Silk was the best-selling soy milk in the country with a leading market share. So the governing statement was straightforward: *Deliver double-digit revenue and profit growth by driving Silk to be a mainstream brand via adult health benefits through soy-based products.*

"In hindsight, our governing statement was too narrow," Kelly Haecker, chief financial officer of WhiteWave, says. "Rather than limiting our focus to soy-based products, we should have broadened our frame to encompass plant-based products in general. Once WhiteWave moved into almond-based milk and other plant-based beverages, stunning results followed. Its overall sales growth accelerated, and Silk is now the number one plant-based beverage in the United States in the soy milk, almond milk, and coconut milk subcategories.

Similarly, the governing statement for Horizon Milk posited *"expanding leadership in premium dairy categories"* rather than encouraging a broader scope of innovation in nondairy alternatives that would be nutritious, better for you, and appeal to Horizon's consumer base. And the governing statement for WhiteWave's dairy and nondairy creamers evolved from a focus on new creamer flavors to include new beverages with iced coffee as a new addition to the product line.

With the TTW process, recurring use of the situation assessment can quickly identify changes that create new key issues and implications that call for revised governing statements and action.

WhiteWave checks its guardrails on a regular basis. The company revisits the situation assessment every year, focusing on what's different, what has changed. It then adjusts its key issues and brand-specific governing statements as needed. "The process forces us to challenge assumptions in a more disciplined way than we might have otherwise," says Kelly. "There are always little tweaks from one year to the next given the changing dynamics in the marketplace.

"Up until now, for example, we've been in plant-based beverages, with the emphasis on beverages. Alpro is our European equivalent of Silk. Going forward, Alpro is starting to teach us to think beyond liquids—to be about plant-based foods and beverages. I think that's the next thing here, too. There's a whole plethora of food opportunities for us—anywhere there's the potential for a dairy proxy," Kelly says.

As with everyone in health services in the United States, a major healthcare insurance provider had to adapt to changes that resulted from the Affordable Care Act. To be responsive to these changes, the human resources function within the company realized it also would have to evolve. The newly appointed chief HR officer saw the need for human resources to transition from a reactive to a proactive role that would better serve its "customers"—other functions within the organization. It needed a new governing statement.

While the HR function had already come a long way from being just the "personnel office," the question was what HR's new role would be, and how best to strengthen and enhance its capabilities.

To define this new participation, the chief HR officer assembled members of her management team and began collecting data and building a SWOT matrix. After looking at both their internal and external environments, they found a number of implications and came to a number of conclusions. Among them was the idea that HR needed to do a better job using data and analysis to inform decision making. It needed not only greater access to data, but also improved analytical capability. The group also identified HR's need for greater efficiency and improved communication, both within the function and with other parts of the organization. Determining that talent management had to become a higher priority within the company, the HR team spelled out a need for greater accountability and for explicit performance and reward standards.

With these and other key conclusions and implications clearly defined, the group was able to put forth a new governing statement that reflected how HR would position itself to its internal customers. It was, in fact, a declaration of intent to become fully integrated into the lifeblood of the company as a whole. It defined its governing statement as: *Deliver world-class HR capabilities through a streamlined, user-friendly model that enables our associates to achieve their business imperatives.*

Getting the Right Balance—Goals Flow from Vision and Governing Statements

Governing statements can be created for teams or working groups of any size and are helpful in unifying a team around a common sense of purpose. During the process, the most important TTW guiding principles we keep in mind are scope (addressing the issue in the appropriate scale) and linkage (connecting the governing statement back to the situation assessment, and forward to goals and measures).

Visions and governing statements respond to the question, How do we position ourselves for success? Goals flow from the answer to that question and the next logical question, which is: What should we aim to achieve? (See Figure 5.2.)

It's been our experience that organizations are too often preoccupied with financial goals and focus on them to the exclusion of all others. Yet the most successful companies have *balanced goals* that address four elements common in virtually every business or institution: people, organization, marketplace, and financial. In Figure 5.3, quadrants 1 and 2—the left side of the matrix—are internal. Quadrants 3 and 4—the right side of the matrix—are external. Both sides should have equal weight.

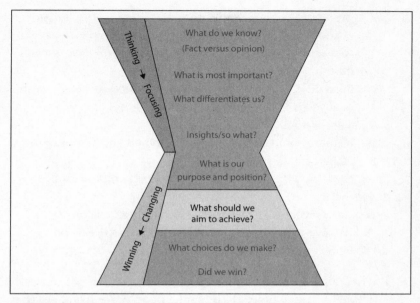

FIGURE 5.2.   WHAT SHOULD WE AIM TO ACHIEVE?

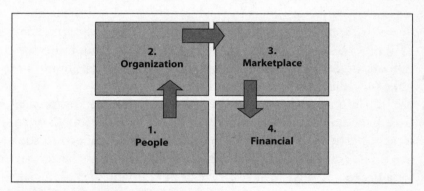

FIGURE 5.3.   BALANCED GOALS MODEL.
Adapted from D. Ulrich, J. Zenger, and N. Smallwood, *Results-Based Leadership*,
Cambridge, MA: Harvard Business School Press, 1999.

These examples will help clarify the need:

1. People:
   - Improve engagement score of all people in our organization by 10 percent next year.
   - Reduce turnover of employees in our company next year by 2 percent.

2. Organization:
   - Maintain zero overhead growth in our expenses associated with selling, general, and administrative items on an annual basis.
   - Build our sales organization to double our distribution reach next year.
3. Marketplace:
   - Increase our market share next year for Brand X from 25 to 30 percent.
   - Grow our international business next year by two times.
4. Financial:
   - Grow revenue by 10 percent a year to $XXX million.
   - Achieve 15 percent contribution margin next year.
   - Reduce our costs by 5 percent a year.

Rather than placing a priority on financials, we actually should start with people. If the right people are in place, they will build the right organization, which will ultimately delight customers and consumers in the marketplace. If all those quadrants are well developed, the money will come—the financials will be in balance. Quadrants 1, 2, and 3 are leading indicators. Quadrant 4 is a lagging indicator. So financial goals should not take precedence over the other three quadrants.

But in our experience, many companies, public and private, small, medium, and large, still focus heavily on that fourth quadrant. That was the case at Gillette before new leadership took over. The company didn't have a strategic plan for the better part of a decade. It did, however, have annual financial goals—with targets that had not been hit for four consecutive years. Gillette was beset by what some described as a "parade of uglies"— 14 straight quarters of missed sales and earnings; constantly declining market shares; drastically curtailed spending on advertising; increased price discounts; excessive cost structure with high and growing overhead, and an insular culture and behaviors.

While many factors perpetuated these uglies, paramount was the top-down declaration of financial goals—goals that were completely divorced from reality. When those financial goals weren't hit, the shortfall was simply added on to the next year's target. As a result, the goals became more extreme and even more divorced from reality year after year. By the time new management came in, they were pure fiction!

The 3Ms: Measures, Metrics, and Milestones

At the time goals are developed, the means by which we will gauge our progress also are established. Some goals can be easily quantified. Others, even if they are less quantifiable, can still be assessed. We refer to these gauges as the *3Ms*: *measures, metrics,* and *milestones*. Each has a role to play:

- ▶ **Measures.** These relate to *what* is involved. It could be that we will gauge our success based on sales, or perhaps earnings will be more important.
- ▶ **Metrics.** These will tell us *how much* we must achieve to be successful. Is it 5 percent in sales growth? Or $2 million in increased earnings?
- ▶ **Milestones.** These tell us *by when* we must act. Fifteen percent increased sales in six months. Or $2 million of increased earnings by year end.

In the same way that we created balanced goals in four quadrants, the 3Ms should likewise be distributed among four quadrants to form a balanced scorecard. An example is shown in Figure 5.4.

A goal must be clear and unambiguous, and the 3Ms also must be explicit. If a goal is vague or if it is described in amorphous terms like "coordinate" or "consider," it will be hard to assess whether it's been attained.

A goal must also be challenging. It should be a stretch, but something that is achievable with excellent effort. The idea of all-out, excellent effort is key. Let's say that one of the fourth quadrant metrics is sales volume. It may be important to guard against a practice that is all too common. In establishing goals, those who will be held accountable for reaching them should have input, but not sole discretion. If the sales organization is unilaterally allowed to declare its own goal, there can be a tendency to set the bar just high enough that it can be achieved with moderate effort. This is an all-too-human tendency. As Michelangelo put it,

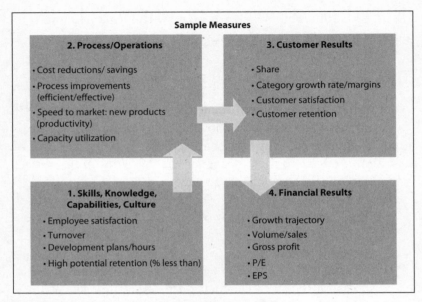

FIGURE 5.4.   THE BALANCED SCORECARD.

"The greater danger for most of us lies not in setting our aim too high and falling short; but in setting our aim too low, and achieving our mark." Setting the bar too low undercuts the essence of a goal—which is that it is something worth reaching for—and the act of reaching is an important part of the motivation process.

Goals that are set too low may produce second-rate effort; goals that are set too high, on the other hand, may yield no effort whatsoever. Impossible goals are demotivators. When people

EMMA'S GOVERNING STATEMENT AND GOALS

Individuals can have governing statements as well. Many of us do—in the form of New Year's resolutions. Too often, however, we don't create the necessary follow-up goals and strategies to see them through.

Emma set herself a governing statement that speaks directly to her quest for a new job:

Position myself to global organizations, headquartered in the northeast United States (ideally in HR) that leverages my core capabilities to achieve personal and professional growth.

Her goals in support of that statement were:

1. To find a new position within six months
2. To obtain her master's degree in under four years
3. To achieve career growth and advancement in 18 months or less

are confronted with them on a regular basis, the incentive to excel disappears and is supplanted by discouragement, often also accompanied by high employee turnover.

Chapter Summary

▶ While the situation assessment in the upper part of the hourglass provides a panoramic view of the present, the vision gives a view of the desired future—what success will look like. It helps clarify what we intend to do to move forward and keeps us from losing our way.

▶ To be effective, a vision must be unique, memorable, and free of jargon, pointing the way to specific strategies, initiatives, and plans. Importantly, to be best in class, vision must tie closely to our SWOT and SCA and be both realizable and actionable.

▶ Governing statement is what we call a vision when it applies to part of a company—like a division or subsidiary—rather than the whole. It also is a guide to the future.

▶ Visions and governing statements respond to the question: How do we position ourselves for success? Goals flow from the answer to that question and the next logical question: How do we define that success?

▶ Balanced goals are best. Too often we get preoccupied with financial goals and focus on them to the exclusion of all others. Yet the greatest success comes with balanced goals that address four elements that are common in virtually every business or institution: people, organization, marketplace, and financial.

▶ Goals that are set too low produce second-rate effort; goals that are too high tend to demotivate and may yield no effort whatsoever.

▶ As goals are developed, the means for gauging progress toward reaching them also are set. Some goals can be easily quantified. Others are less quantifiable, but can still be assessed. The key gauges are the 3Ms: measures, metrics, and milestones.

Chapter 5 Exercises

What Is Our Purpose and Position?

We need to focus on governing statements.

Mastering Governing Statements

The governing statement is the overall objective for the business. It helps to set the scope and parameters of "where the business operates."

A governing statement should ask the following:

▶ Where is our focus?—direction of energy; where the organization should "play" (operate).
▶ How/where should the business competitively position itself in the marketplace?
▶ What are our guardrails? What we are *not* going to do to compromise our competitive advantage?

Creating Governing Statements

Step 1: Review the context:
  ● Individually reflect on the context: Ask yourself: What do I know? What is most important? How are we unique? What differentiates us?
Step 2: Draft your statement considering the following (note: this should be no more than two sentences):
  ● What is our overarching objective?
  ● What is our position? (Where do we play? What is the role we play?)
  ● Are we providing a clear point of view?
  ● Place it on the wall for all to see.
Step 3: Share your statement:
  ● Read your statement to others.

- Questions that seek to clarify are the only ones that should be asked at this point: "What does that mean?"

Step 4: Dialogue:

- Collectively ask, What do we see?
- Where are there similarities? Differences? At this point we find that there are pretty similar statements—it is not brainstorming but a convergent exercise.
- Identify and circle key words/phrases.

Step 5: Work from the statement that most closely represents all points of view:

- Align on the statement that represents the best point of view.
- Assign two or three people to draft the final statement for others to approve.

Tip: Ask an unbiased source to read the statement without any context and ask that person to define the issue. If the statement is clear enough, he or she will be able to identify each element and understand what needs to be addressed.

What Should We Aim to Achieve? How Will We Know If We "Win"?

We need to create and master smart goals.

Mastering Smart Goals

There are two principles when it comes to developing goals: SMART and balanced.

SMART is an acronym for significant, measurable, achievable, relevant, and time-bound. The best way to make sure goals are well written is to focus on the "M" in SMART. We expand this through the 3M methodology: measures, metrics, and milestones. Ask the following:

- ▶ **Measures.** What must we identify: sales, profit, market share, turnover, and so on?
- ▶ **Metrics.** How much? What is the metric? Numbers? Percentage increase?
- ▶ **Milestones.** By when? When should this be accomplished (months, years, and so on?)

We believe the best way to achieve this result is with what we call a *balanced scorecard*. Ask the following:

▶ Are we too preoccupied with financial goals? Are we focused on them to the exclusion of all other goals?
▶ Do we have balanced goals that address the four elements common to virtually every business or institution: people, organization, marketplace, and financial? These elements are illustrated in Figure 5.5.

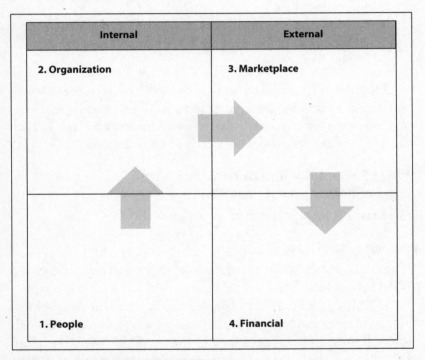

Internal	External
2. Organization	**3. Marketplace**
1. People	**4. Financial**

FIGURE 5.5. BALANCED MATRIX.

Exercise: Creating Goals

This exercise can be done at an individual or group level.

1. Create a goal statement for each quadrant of the scorecard.
2. Using the information provided, determine the appropriate measures, metrics, and milestones for each goal by answering the following questions:
   a. What is the correct measure?

   b. What are realistic targets?
   c. What is the appropriate timing?
3. Hold a discussion with key stakeholders for:
   a. Clarity
   b. Aligning on goals

The deliverable will be balanced goals with measures, metrics, and milestones identified and aligned.

Organizational Assessment

Use the following table as a checklist for identifying TTW principles and practices. This will help you to better understand where you and your team need to focus your energies. To get an idea where you believe your organization stands, read through each statement and jot down a rating:

Concept/Process	Scale: 1 = Low, 5 = High
Our company has established measurable goals and targets, as well as timelines for us to realistically expect results.	
Our goals are comprehensive, addressing four stakeholder groups: people, organization, marketplace, and financial.	
We are clearly able to articulate our company's vision statement.	
We have plans in place to adjust, track, and monitor our goals.	
We use our governing statements to position the organization for success.	

Review individual items. Look for items on which you scored lower (3 and below) and think about the following questions:

► What do I believe is driving the score?
► What do I need to stop, start, or continue doing?
► What do I hope the result to be?

CHAPTER 6

Strategies: Making the Right Choices

What happens when you have a coffee making system that's selling like gangbusters because of its exclusive, patented features, but its patent is about to expire? And your competitors will soon be able to copy your product and invade your market.

Answer: You spend a lot of sleepless nights while you work tirelessly on assessing the possible approaches, the possible strategies for how to deal with the issue, perhaps the most important issue ever for the company.

And that's what *strategies* are all about. They're the options and choices we must make when deciding how to achieve our goals. Choose the right strategy and we have a clear path to success. Choose the wrong one, and we'll quickly be checkmated.

Fortunately, while the stakes are high, we've already done much of the work for developing and selecting strategies since they flow from our efforts in the top half of the hourglass—from our SWOT, SCA, and key issue identification. Basically, we start by asking the right questions:

- ▶ What do we do well that the market would value?
- ▶ What unanswered needs exist in our market?
- ▶ What would it take to become the market leader in this market?

There's a lot to consider, but our SWOT and SCA will help us decide where we should focus our attention—the right mix of factors such as where to "play"—the region or geographic area; what product categories, customer segments, and distribution channels to consider; and how our strengths and advantages can enhance our ability to win (see Figure 6.1).

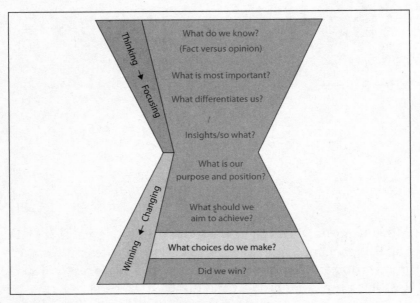

FIGURE 6.1.   WHAT CHOICES DO WE MAKE?

Aha Moments and Insights Inspire Strategies

To generate a list of possible strategies, we have several good approaches for you to pursue. We have found that many options originate with the aha moments we experience in the top of the hourglass. Those insights inspire novel ways of looking at a problem, and they can do the same for developing strategies.

Since we want a range of strategies to assess, we also can brainstorm to help ensure that we have both diversity and quantity. Brainstorming has been called a method for creating an idea explosion, a creativity bomb of unfiltered, unevaluated, uncensored possibilities. (See the sidebar for details on this approach.)

The goal of all approaches is to generate a set of core strategies plus possible alternative approaches.

BRAINSTORMING STRATEGIC OPTIONS

Brainstorming on strategic options may bring together an unlikely cast of characters, especially if the culture of the organization is primarily left-brained or heavily risk-averse. If what is needed is disruptive innovation, the best people for the task may be your in-house disruptive innovators. In lieu of the CEO, the CFO, and a few direct reports, the brainstorming session could include the CEO, the fashionista from marketing, the brilliant geek from R&D, the bright new hire in HR, and a facilitator.

The job of the facilitator is to move the process along and keep everyone focused on the problem. He or she may be a company employee or an outside professional. Facilitators set the ground rules and then make sure that everyone sticks to them and remains focused on the problem. Even if the boss's boss is in the room, the facilitator will find a way to remind everyone—nicely, of course—to check both their egos and their chevrons at the door.

The job of the group is to solve the problem, and given that assignment, there should be no such thing as a bad idea. This is not the time for self-censorship—it is not unusual for one participant to take another's "crazy idea," tweak it slightly, and come up with a winning possibility. The goal of the session is to generate strategies.

These strategies will almost always include one that says let's stay the course, or stay the course with a few incremental adjustments. But they also should include several bolder choices. These "outside the box" options will more than likely cause upheaval and may take years to achieve, but that doesn't mean they should be off the table.

Undertaking a major course correction may be necessary to avoid being leapfrogged or sidetracked by aggressive competitors or by factors occurring in the marketplace. The choice by WhiteWave to move beyond soy-based products into almond and other plant-based products is a good example. The choice by New Balance to add a line of clothing and open its own stores is another.

Before we look at how we cull through our options and narrow down and finalize our choices, let's look at Keurig and its strategic challenge of facing patent expiration.

Confronting Patent Expiration

By 2008, the Keurig single-cup coffeemaker had started its meteoric rise in popularity. People were captivated by the simplicity, convenience, and quality: pop a K-Cup Pack into the brewer, push a button, and get a consistently high-quality cup of coffee in minutes. Despite the recession, the parent company Keurig Green Mountain was growing at an amazing 70 percent compound growth rate.

Scaling up to keep pace with the growth was itself a problem. "Our management team knew we would have to almost double our workforce in 18 months," says former president Michelle Stacy, "which meant we would have to hire potentially 200 people within 12 months . . . and that meant interviewing six times as many people —three candidates for each role, and two rounds of interviews for each one. A total of 1,800 interviews. Looking at what it would take just to keep up with the hiring, we were stunned."

But Keurig's HR group figured out how many recruiters it would need, and streamlined the procedure to minimize the amount of time spent on the interviewing. "We thought we were so smart," says Michelle with a laugh, "We were doing a great job hiring—we had the whole thing down. And then I walked in one day and found two people sitting in a broom closet. Somewhere in the process, we'd completely forgotten that if you hire that many people, they need a place to sit. We were out of space. Next thing I knew, our CEO asked us to develop a plan for a new corporate headquarters in the Boston area."

Running out of room and hiring new employees, however, were not the problems that kept Michelle and her team awake at night. Even though the company was growing rapidly, there was a huge potential problem on the horizon. The patent on their exclusive single-cup brewing system would expire in 2012. The company needed to make sure that its sustainable competitive advantage was not reliant entirely on the patent. It needed strategies and competencies that would extend its SCA on multiple fronts.

"In 2008, we were very aware that this was coming at us," Michelle says. "The choice of what we would do was one of the biggest decisions we would ever make. What strategies could we deploy to minimize the impact of losing our patent exclusivity? We laid out three options:

- ▶ What would happen if we did nothing?
- ▶ What would happen if we put a new brewing system in place under a different patent?
- ▶ What would happen if we brought in partners?

Michelle and her team then went back to their situation assessment for guidance and their key insight came when they took a closer look at their business from the consumer's perspective.

Many experts had been puzzled by Keurig's success. Beginning as a tiny start-up, it wasn't the first to market with a single-serving coffeemaker. Analysts struggled to explain why Keurig had done so much better, even when it was competing head-to-head with bigger, more powerful adversaries like Nestle's Nespresso brand.

"When we looked at our business from the consumer's point of view, it came down to two reasons," says Michelle. "The first is that the American consumer wants to drink 10 to 12 ounces of coffee in one sitting. Most of the other machines, including the ones that were ahead of us in the market, were based on the European preference for six ounces. Six ounces of coffee is not enough for the U.S. consumer, and watering down a good six-ounce cup with four ounces of water to get to 10 ounces is not the right answer. Ours was the first system that delivered eight to 12 ounces of coffee that really tasted good."

The second reason was that American consumers wanted to have a choice. "Every other system was 'my machine—my coffee,'" Michelle explains. "Keurig Green Mountain was different. We established relationships with other coffee roasters, so consumers didn't feel locked in. For us it was '*our machine—our coffee plus all these other possibilities*.' Initially, we worked with several smaller brands. But consumers liked choice, so we decided expanding our partnering strategy was our best option."

And the Keurig Green Mountain team members made the right choice. They found that the more variety they offered, the more consumers loved their system. Keurig Green Mountain eventually brokered partnership arrangements with Dunkin' Donuts and Starbucks and many other coffee and beverage makers. It was Keurig's pathway into mainstream acceptance, and it was one of the keys to sustaining growth after the patents expired.

"Extending ourselves through our partners created a network of coffee brands. We might have lost a little short-term profit, but we gained long-term profitability. Nevertheless, it was a tremendous risk," Michelle says. "We were inviting the competition into our proprietary systems. You can imagine what it was like to sit across from our own Green Mountain Coffee brand manager and say, 'By the way, we're going to Starbucks next week, because we think we need the Starbucks and Dunkin' Donut brands in the system.' Those discussions were gut-wrenching, but the partnerships really were the right choice for the business."

"All of those companies that came in as partners with us before we came off the patent stayed with us as partners after we came off the patent," says Michelle. "And we never went over that cliff that so many expected."

Winning Beyond Patents

The process of weighing these options and making such a momentous decision also prompted Michelle and her team to go back and reconsider what Keurig Green Mountain's sustainable competitive advantage really was. If it wasn't the patent, what was it? "We asked ourselves, 'What did we have that nobody else can get to?'" she says, "and we realized that what we had was more than just being protected by patents. We had the collective know-how to make the system work. We knew our consumers. We knew who they were and what they wanted. We had a unique relationship with them. We owned the way the brewer functioned, how it heated, the algorithms that are in it to heat and then pressurize the water to deliver a great cup of coffee. We owned how to make the portion pack, and we owned the connection between the brewer and the pack. The knowledge of how to do that, and how to do it with ease, was really our sustainable competitive advantage."

Keurig's success in developing, assessing, and acting on strategic options over the years was evidenced by the phenomenal shareholder value it created. The company also received a vote of confidence when the Coca-Cola Company purchased 16 percent of the firm's equity and signed a joint agreement for Keurig to sell many of Coke's cold refreshment beverages in Keurig's unique in-home/in-office cold beverage brewer.

Zeroing In on the Right Choices

Choosing the best strategy begins with having the right set of options to select from. But how do we know which strategy or set of strategies to select? Narrowing the list of options again involves asking a series of questions to see which approaches seem most likely to present a winning solution. For example, what conditions would have to be in place for us to be confident of this possibility? Are those conditions in place now, or could they be put in place? Do we have adequate facts and data to feel confident about the approach? Would the approach yield significant enough results to move us toward our goal?

As we go through these questions, we can further assess which factors are *essential,* or *must-haves,* and which are helpful but not indispensable.

Once we've assessed the value of our different options, then we have to gauge the degree of difficulty in carrying them out. In other words, what are the *enablers* and *barriers* to each option? For enablers, are they now in place or could they be created in a timely, affordable fashion? For barriers, what would be the degree of difficulty in eliminating or overcoming them? If the enablers are in place and the potential barriers can be quickly overcome, the choice is likely to be sound. If barriers exist and we're unsure whether they can be surmounted, then further review and testing is necessary.

Once we've finalized our likely strategies, we ask some additional questions to confirm our selection. Can we link our strategies to particular goals? Do they leverage our sustainable competitive advantage(s)? When implemented would the strategies deliver results and impact to meet our goals and address our key issues?

At this time, we also make note of the strategies we considered, but discarded. These may prove useful in the future, especially if conditions change. These ideas not only form a group of options-in-waiting, but also help sharpen the ability to explain the chosen strategy to others. It is always important to have contingency strategies, a "plan B," in the event our strategies don't work or can't be implemented.

Let's see now how a midsized company approached its strategic choices as it viewed a market where demographics, trends, brand image, and consumer preferences all had started moving against it.

Dramatic Market Change Dictates Dramatic Strategic Shift

When a cosmetics and skin-care company that we'll call BetterFace, Inc. considered its options to address the dramatic changes revealed in its situation assessment, it developed and discarded several alternative strategies before committing to four core strategies that would transform its business. As we'll see, each of the accepted strategies was chosen by considering how well it matched BetterFace's strengths, filled market needs, and could overcome barriers.

BetterFace made and marketed low- and moderate-priced cosmetics and skin-care products in chain drugstores and department stores. They also made upscale brands and store brands that sold through specialty channels, including home-shopping television, cosmetics-only shops, spas, beauty and skin-care salons, designer boutiques, and online.

After an extensive situation assessment, it produced the SWOT shown in Table 6.1.

For BetterFace, the greatest urgency was the need to pivot in response to rapidly changing market conditions. Boomer and Gen Y women, who comprise the core of its spa and home shopping market clientele, were shifting away from purchasing eye, cheek, and lip color, and instead were investing in skin-care products that hold off the appearance of aging. Unfortunately, BetterFace lacked a strong positive image with millennials—young women who could offset the anticipated losses among older women. To them, BetterFace made products for their mothers, aunts, and grandmothers.

TABLE 6.1. BETTERFACE, INC.

Strengths	Opportunities
▶ Track record of successful product innovation ▶ Excellent marketing connections between our reps and their customers ▶ Great makeup, lots of choices that appeal to a diverse group of women ▶ Heavy presence in spas and skin-care salons. ▶ Strong history of recommendations by estheticians in skin-care salons	▶ Boomers and Gen Y shoppers, both men and women, poised to invest more in skin-care products. ▶ Affluent older women (Whole Foods Boomers) and college educated younger women (Grass-roots Millennials) trending strongly toward preference for natural or organic products ▶ Latina market growing in size and affluence ▶ Individualization—diminishing power of "one size fits all" definition of beauty
Weaknesses	**Threats**
▶ Lack of in-house knowledge of state-of-the-art science in natural cosmetic and skin-care formulation ▶ Lack of presence in dermatologist/laser treatment facilities compared to competitors ▶ Lack of buzz compared to our competitors with younger women—shortage of word-of-mouth recommendations from beauty bloggers, campus reviewers, etc.	▶ Brand associated with cosmetics, not skin care ▶ "Dowdy" image with millennials ▶ Emergence of smaller innovators capitalizing on perceived weakness of larger players ▶ Increased safety regulations and consumer awareness of cosmetic impurities (crushed cochineal bugs in red lipstick, plastic microbeads in face wash, etc.)

Perhaps worse, BetterFace may have trouble hanging onto that core older generation, since its skin-care line has long taken a back seat to its brightly colored, higher-profit lines of lipsticks, eye shadows, and blushers. BetterFace has been known as a company that is skin deep.

It has a great reputation as a maker of a broad range of quality cosmetics that disguise or cover up flaws, wrinkles, and blemishes. It is not known as a maker of healthy, good-for-you products that make women look and feel beautiful from the inside out, nor does it have a particularly strong reputation for antiaging products. During the situation assessment, BetterFace confirmed this from survey research, but it is also echoed in the SWOT by the difference between its relative strength among estheticians in skin-care and beauty salons and its very low profile among clinicians in dermatological offices.

Strategies—No Longer Skin Deep

For BetterFace, the key takeaway from the analysis in the upper half of the hourglass is the imperative to escape the negative consequences of its "skin deep" reputation. To do so, it will have to greatly expand its skin-care line and cultivate a much stronger reputation as skin-care experts. Because the market is fragmenting by age, by ethnicity, and by skin type, it also needs to leverage its capacity for product innovation to develop product lines that appeal specifically to particular market segments: millennials, Latinas, and Asians.

In response, BetterFace produced the following vision statement: *BetterFace: We love the skin you're in.*

It set goals that included the following marketplace targets:

▶ Grow skin-care net sales by 10 percent per year for the next three years.
▶ Grow millennial market share by 5 percent per year for the next three years.
▶ Grow Latina market share by 4 percent per year for the next three years.

The question was how best to proceed. To reach those goals, BetterFace adopted a number of strategies in direct response to both marketplace opportunities and to serious threats:

▶ **Strategy 1: Develop enhanced skin-care capability; expand skin-care offerings.** This strategy, addressing a SWOT weakness, could be implemented either by rapid development of this capability in-house, or by acquisition of another company with skin-care expertise.
▶ **Strategy 2: Launch organic skin-care line with natural ingredients.** This strategy is dependent on the implementation of strategy 1. With organically sourced ingredients and recyclable

packaging, it has the potential to span the generation gap, appealing both to "Whole Foods Boomers," and "Grass-roots Millennials." This strategy also addresses a SWOT weakness.

▶ **Strategy 3: Launch Latina cosmetics and skin-care line.** This strategy would require development of a strong presence in Spanish language media, but also presents the future possibility of international sales in Central and South America. Given the traditional strong family ties in Latino families, promotion for this strategy is expected to stress the connection between mothers and daughters, both using the new line, but with products tailored specifically for each age group. The SWOT identifies the growing and increasingly affluent Latina market as an opportunity.

▶ **Strategy 4: Launch millennial promotional campaign.** This strategy would utilize social media to reintroduce BetterFace to younger women. It would also entail working through college-level social and professional organizations, which are predominantly female (sororities, nursing schools, elementary education programs) to distribute sample products and discount coupons. To implement this strategy, outsourcing would be needed to secure social media expertise.

Focus on the Vital Few

Also important to consider are the approaches rejected by BetterFace. The first was the "stay the course" option, which would have entailed minimal to moderate refinements to its business plan. If analysis in the top half of the hourglass had not shown such dramatic changes, this default approach of business as usual with some tweaks and adjustments might have been an option. But the SWOT made it clear that greater changes were essential.

Also rejected was the development of a Boomer men's brand to parallel the aging skin-care line being developed for women. Men's face-care products in general follow women's trends; they do not precede them or even run concurrent with them. Once BetterFace had successfully launched its FreshFace brand for women, it would take another look at adding a men's line.

A strategy to launch a separate millennial line also was deferred. After much discussion, BetterFace felt that adding another new line would overtax internal capabilities. So too was the option to launch a brand appealing specifically to Asian women. The market potential was not considered large enough, except on the West Coast. But the option would be revisited in the future if more new demographic information justified it.

CHOICES FOR EMMA

Emma established strategies for each of her stated goals.

1. *Goal:* To find a new position within six months
   Strategic Option: (1) Focus on networking with HR executives, (2) Conduct information interviews with people in target companies
2. *Goal:* To obtain her master's degree in under four years
   Strategic Option: (1) Attend a New England school that has strong reputation for business, (2) Attend part time while working— choose an executive MBA program that meets budget needs
3. *Goal:* To achieve career growth and advancement in 18 months or less
   Strategic Option: (1) Choose an organization that has a management development program, (2) Ensure that the hiring manager has a bias toward mentoring and people development

There are two strategic options that Emma considers but rejects. The first is to retain a job search specialist (headhunter) to help her find and apply for positions. She researches the cost, and their average rate of success for professionals at her level of advancement, and determines that she could do at least as well herself. She also chooses not to take a hiatus from work in order to study full time to achieve her graduate degree. Even though it will take her longer to get her masters if she works while studying, she decides the ability to immediately use what she's learning is worth the extra time it would take to complete the program.

Chapter Summary

▶ The daunting prospect of making a choice, deciding on the right strategies to pursue to achieve our goals, is made easy by the work done at the top of the hourglass.

- Many strategic options flow directly from the insights and aha moments already experienced.
- Our SWOT and SCA further guide our assessment and selection process since focus on our strengths and abilities to overcome weaknesses and barriers inform our choices.
- Developing a robust list of options ensures comprehensive thinking, helps secure team alignment, and also provides contingency options for the future.

Chapter 6 Exercises

What Choices Do We Make?

Mastering TTW Choices

Strategies are about choices. They answer the questions: Where do we play? and How do we win? They are the means to an end. Strategies need to be significant, have major impact, and be comprehensive enough to achieve the goal.

Start by asking:

- How do we determine our best set of options? How do we develop strategic alternatives, and how do we know which to select?
- What do we do well that the market might value?
- What would it take to be the next Facebook, Apple, Amazon, and Walmart in this space? Where do we focus our efforts on the 10 percent of strategies that will deliver 90 percent of the wins? (See A. G. Lafley, R. Martin, J. W. Rivkin, and N. Siggelow, "Bringing Science to the Art of Strategy," *Harvard Business Review*, September 2012.)

Exercise: Identifying Strategic Options
(Can be done at individual or group level)

1. Paying close attention to our implications and governing statements, brainstorm the strategic options: where to play (consider geographies, product categories, customer segments, channels we can add, market value) and how to win (consider our strengths and SCAs).

2. Create a list of statements—consolidate into four to six using the following criteria:
   a. Leverage strengths
   b. Addresses marketplace opportunities
   c. Linkage to vision, governing statements, and goals
   d. Capability
   e. Customer/consumer demand
3. What are the conditions for success? What would have to be true for me to be confident in this possibility? (Example: Top two customers would have to support us, or consumers would trade up to a higher price point.)
4. For each strategic option that you are considering you will need to assess what is potentially getting in the way of the option becoming a strategic choice.
5. Have a conversation with other stakeholders to clarify and gain alignment.

The deliverable is a draft of strategic priorities.

You need to develop three different levels of strategies: core, alternative, and contingent. Your core strategy is what you will recommend based on the analysis in the top of the hourglass. Alternative strategies were actively considered, but ultimately rejected in favor of the core strategy. They are important because even though conditions are not right for them at this time, they may become your core strategies in the future. Your contingency strategy is your plan B. This backup plan is essential, in case the initial core strategies don't work or become unavailable.

Organizational Assessment

Use the following table below as a checklist for identifying TTW principles and practices. This will help you to better understand where you and your team need to focus your energies. To get an idea where you believe your organization stands, read through each statement and jot down a rating:

Concept/Process	Scale: 1 = Low, 5 = High
Our strategies are clear choices that are based upon thorough analyses and insights.	
We are able to clearly articulate the strategic choices we need to make to support our goals.	
Our organization's current strategies give us a clear advantage over the competition.	
We identify what conditions for success are necessary before we land on a strategy.	
We are able to articulate why we reject a strategic choice.	

Review individual items. Look for items on which you scored lower (3 and below) and think about the following questions:

- ▶ What do I believe is driving the score?
- ▶ What do I need to stop, start, or continue doing?
- ▶ What do I hope the result to be?

Confronting the Elusive: Moving from Planning to Acting

Failure to execute plans is a virtually universal problem. So why is the solution to the problem so elusive?

Legendary executive Larry Bossidy, whose career as a senior executive at General Electric and CEO of Honeywell defined excellence, says failure to execute plagues almost all businesses large and small. The ability to move from thinking and planning to acting and accomplishing challenges everyone.

In *Execution: The Discipline of Getting Things Done* (New York: Crown Books, 2002), the book Bossidy coauthored with the globally renowned consultant Ram Charan, he says: "When companies fail to deliver on their promises, the most frequent explanation is that the CEO's strategy was wrong. But the strategy itself is not the cause. Strategies most often fail because they aren't executed well. Things that are supposed to happen don't happen. Either the organizations aren't capable of making them happen, or the leaders of the business misjudge the challenges their companies face in the business environment, or both."

And the Project Management Institute affirms these beliefs. In a 2013 research paper titled "Why Good Strategies Fail: Lessons for the C-Suite," the institute found that even though 88 percent of executives surveyed are convinced that carrying out strategic plans must be a priority, their own companies are not following through. More than 60 percent admitted that their organizations had trouble converting strategy formulation into strategy implementation. Over a recent three-year period, almost half of all initiatives had not succeeded.

So this raises the question we started with: If failure is so universal, why is the solution so elusive?

Bossidy proposes a tripartite answer. Execution fails because it's not approached with the necessary discipline; it's not embraced as the top leader's responsibility, and it's not a part of the organization's culture.

We agree, but we also know that TTW offers some simple approaches that can make a big difference in successfully moving from think to win to acting to succeed.

Let's start with two TTW concepts: First, the importance of how action rooted in the situation assessment phase of TTW facilitates the flow from planning to action; and second, how teams can be a significant factor.

A solid umbrella statement that leads to a robust and relevant situation assessment actually contains the seeds of the initiatives that are the basis for execution. If tight linkage exists throughout the planning phase, execution becomes seamless.

The way to make sure things happen is through teams, whether they are formal or informal. Strategies get executed by the work people do. They work on projects; they work on tasks; and they work together as teams. To be successful, we must ask specific people to do specific things. Initiatives are these specifics, and people carrying them out should have a clear understanding of how their efforts are connected to what the company is trying to achieve. Each initiative needs to be aligned with a particular strategy, as shown in Figure 7.1.

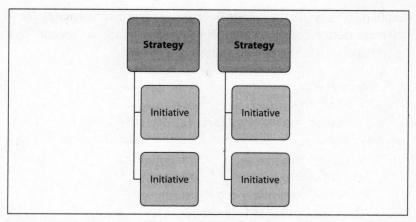

FIGURE 7.1.   ALIGN ALL ACTIONS WITH STRATEGIES.

Putting Teams in Place

In this composite, Steve is the new brand manager for THRIVE organic baby foods. The brand has been struggling, and now sits far behind Beech-Nut and Gerber. Steve's corporate executives tell him that the first priority for the division is to grow market share. Having put THRIVE through an extensive situation assessment and SWOT analysis, Steve and his team identify THRIVE's strong positioning and market strength with Latino families as a sustainable competitive advantage (SCA). Latinos will account for more than half of all population growth for many years; more than one in four children will be born each year into Hispanic households. Surveys show that Latino parents have a strong and growing preference for organic baby foods, and they are willing to pay more for them. Moreover, their survey responses indicate that parents are disappointed in the flavor choices available. This was a place where THRIVE believed it could play and win—an avenue for growth that it made the choice to exploit.

So Steve puts together a team to plan the execution. He tapped four colleagues from various departments in the division. Having Latino voices on the team was a priority, as was having people who had been through the parenting experience. At their first meeting, they established their team charter, which was specific to this initiative and contained six elements: membership, assumptions, significance/objectives, interdependencies, longer-term deliverables, and timing/communication. Several key questions help define each element:

1. Membership:
   - Who is the sponsor?
   - Who is the core team, team leader, team facilitator?
   - What is the transition plan for team members over the life of the initiative?

2. Assumptions:
   - What do we assume to be true?
   - What is in place that we can use?

3. Significance/objectives:
   - What is the significance of the initiative to the business?
   - What is the initiative intended to accomplish, and what will signal success?
   - What are the quantifiable targets of the initiative?
   - What are the longer-term deliverables?

4. Interdependencies:
   - Who are the stakeholders necessary for success?
   - Who else do we depend on for products, ideas, and information who are not on the team?
   - Who do we need to keep in the loop?
   - Where is work already being done?

5. Short- and long-term deliverables:
   - What do we need to deliver in the next 30, 60, or 90 days?
   - What will we deliver over the next one to three years?
   - What will help sustain our success?

6. Timing/communication:
   - What is the anticipated initiative duration?
   - What is the plan and schedule for keeping the sponsors, steering committee, core team, functional managers, and other key stakeholders involved and informed?

As we can see from Figure 7.2, the charter Steve's team developed spells out the details—who are involved, who are tangentially connected, and what they are going to produce in both the short and long term.

Membership:
- Sponsor: CEO
- Leader: Steve
- Team members: Eddie, Elena, Carlos, Patrick
- Timing: Quick screen, December—deep dive to follow

Assumptions:
- Supply is available
- Work will be done in two phases: Quick screen and ongoing systems /processes
- Need to look at broader "competition"—who else is trying to grow in this space?

Significance and objectives:
- Scope is THRIVE organic baby foods
- Assess the situation—what do we see in the next 12 months?
- What is the best way to launch?

Interdependencies:
- Supply team
- Marketing

Long-Term Deliverables
- Integrate new product into a sustained campaign targeting the Latino family
- Current strategies give us a clear advantage over the competition

Short-Term Deliverables
- Three new flavors rolled out over the coming calendar year
- Assessment of competitive challenges

FIGURE 7.2.   WORKING GROUP: GROW LATINO MARKET SHARE.

MAKING DECISIONS! DON'T COMPLICATE IT— THINK TO WIN!

It is important that team members have a real voice in the definition of initiatives and in the determination of who will have responsibility for seeing them to completion. That said, although debate and perhaps even controversy about the actions are to be expected, there should be no controversy about how the group makes those decisions. As part of its structure, the team needs to establish ground rules for decision making, and do so *before* there are important choices on the table. We suggest that the group use the following process when making a choice on what actions to undertake.

1. Name or label the decision that needs to be made. Make sure wording is clear and precise.
2. Discuss how the decision relates to the "big picture," the higher purpose of the issue.
3. Discuss implications.

(Continues)

4. Align—can we get behind this (team/sponsors/stakeholders)?
5. Vote—majority rule/tiebreaker to leader.
6. Declare agreement and commitment.
7. Communicate in writing.

The first step, being clear on what is to be decided and giving it a name, may sound obvious. But too often this can be where problems begin. With a complex issue, or with multiple participants speaking different languages (HR, R&D, marketing, finance), misunderstandings may arise among colleagues about what the choice actually entails. The second step is to be mindful of why the choice matters. It's useful to rely on the team charter—invoke the higher purpose, the greater goal—to help motivate people to get aligned. Because obtaining unanimity on every decision is highly unlikely, it is generally the wiser course of action to seek alignment rather than agreement.

The technique used to obtain alignment often can make a difference. We have found one simple technique to be quite effective. Instead of a show of hands, try a show of *thumbs*. When a decision is to be made, if your thumb is up, you're behind it. If your thumb is sideways, you're not thrilled, but you can live with it and are willing to move forward. If your thumb is down, you're not aligned, which means you then have the floor to communicate your objections and reservations. The person running the meeting encourages the speaker to be as specific as possible in describing what is troubling about the decision, and what alternatives might be preferable. In the dialogue that ensues, it is often the case that after several minutes of talking it out, many of those thumbs-down turn at least horizontal. Even if someone remains opposed, however, the discussion has value, both in getting everything out on the table, and in giving colleagues the chance to be heard.

The most common voting technique is majority rule: if the thumbs-ups and the thumbs-horizontals outnumber the thumbs-downs, they carry the day. If the votes are evenly split, the team leader holds the tiebreaker. An alternative voting system, however, may be appropriate in some circumstances. If the decision to be made has major consequences, for example, serious health or safety implications for colleagues or consumers, the group may take a more conservative approach. Rather than majority rule, this voting system might be called No trumps Yes, where a single negative vote serves as a veto. Under these ground rules, every thumb would have to be at least horizontal to move forward. Whichever voting system is deployed, after the vote has been taken and a group decision has been made, every outcome should be recorded and declared in writing. At that point, it no longer matters how each individual voted—everyone on the team must commit to the collective decision. The team or working group needs to speak with one voice to its colleagues in the rest of the company and beyond.

Review the Choices

With their charter set and with increasing market share among Latinos as their target, Steve and his team must decide how to leverage their SCA. They faced a difficult challenge. Not only were they up against formidable competitors, but the overall category, with the exception of the Latino market, was declining. They needed one or more initiatives that would deliver a bigger slice of a shrinking pie.

The strategy was to grow market share through targeted products for the Latino market. Initiatives to be considered included:

▶ Develop and market three new organic products based on classic Caribbean and Central American flavors.
▶ Increase advertising on Spanish language radio and television.
▶ Improve product placement in bodegas and local markets.
▶ Develop separate brand with Spanish labeling.

How would Steve and his team choose among them? By thinking them through. As always with TTW, the key is asking the right questions:

▶ **Degree of impact on strategy:** How much of the strategy would be satisfied by the successful completion of the initiative?

► **Organizational readiness:** Is the organization currently a help or a hindrance to the successful completion of the initiative?
► **Capabilities:** Does the organization have the skills, experience, and know-how to drive the initiative?

Steve and his team debated the relative merits of each initiative and then ranked them, using a simple scale of 1 to 3 to gauge their degree of impact: 1 = low, 2 = medium, or 3 = high. The higher the degree of impact, the more likely they would be to commit to the initiative. These were the results:

► Develop and market three new products based on classic Caribbean and Central American flavors: 3
► Increase advertising on Spanish language radio and television: 2
► Improve product placement in bodegas and local markets: 1
► Develop separate brand with Spanish language labeling: 2

Since the third initiative was rated as having low impact, it was eliminated in favor of the remaining initiatives that had more potential.

Steve already knew that the team dialogue about ranking had a value all its own that was almost as important as the ranking itself. A focused discussion about the merits of the various initiatives, with input from the entire team, is often a major step toward securing buy-in from the colleagues who would carry them out. The interchange among team members can also help shape the mindset of the unit as a whole.

During an intense debate about the merits of a direct appeal to ethnicity, two team members convinced fellow members that the approach would be insensitive and too blunt. They argued that it would be a poor choice. The best way to reach Latina women, they said, would be to approach them as mothers, talk about the mother-baby connection, and connect with their strong desires to raise healthy children. This insight was also useful in developing a promotional campaign for the new products.

Steve and his team then considered the next key question: How ready is your organization to carry out the initiative?

In other words, what barriers would potentially block its success, and what boosters or enablers would help? They found two potential difficulties and two sources of support, and ranked them on the same 1 to 3 scale. (See Table 7.1.)

TABLE 7.1. ORGANIZATIONAL READINESS: DEVELOP AND MARKET THREE NEW PRODUCTS BASED ON CLASSIC CARIBBEAN AND CENTRAL AMERICAN FLAVORS

Potential Barriers	Degree of Impact on Initiative
▶ Cost of initiative is high	▶ 3
▶ Supply uncertainty	▶ 3
Potential Enablers	**Degree of Impact on Initiative**
▶ Senior management is very supportive	▶ 3
▶ In-house experience exists	▶ 2

As with ranking potential impact, team dialogue on barriers and enablers also has merit and can form the basis for constructive discussion on whether to proceed with the initiative. In general, barriers carry more weight than enablers. Steve realized that it was likely they would proceed with the initiative and would ask the team to develop a plan to both leverage the enablers and reduce the barriers.

Steve and his team then considered whether the company had the necessary skills and experience to support the initiative. If not, could it readily obtain them? Without capability, neither the initiatives nor the strategies they support will succeed. Steve realized that for this initiative to be successful, it would be imperative to lock down a secure supply of tropical fruit, including mangos, guavas, and plantains. The team determined that although it would be preferable to designate someone within THRIVE to be responsible for this task, it would be faster and more efficient to job it out to an independent supplier.

For initiatives that require a specialized skill, in-house capability is usually preferable. But if that capability is lacking, it may take a long time and serious investment to develop. When time is a critical factor, "growing your own" may not be feasible. When the New Balance running shoe company decided to add a clothing line, senior leadership realized that expertise in apparel did not exist in-house and could not be developed quickly enough to fit the desired time frame. To execute that strategy, New Balance chose instead to acquire another company that already had experience in manufacturing and marketing athletic wear. When outside know-how needs to be imported, the cost of bringing in these skills ought to be determined at the outset.

Identify and Manage the Initiatives

Once initiatives are selected, they must be managed. There are three factors to keep in mind: *scope, time,* and *costs.* Initiatives have size and features. They are time bound. And they consume money and resources. These are the triple trade-offs, and they are completely interdependent. Like three meshed gears, if one turns, they all turn. If one goes off kilter, they all stop. A further look at our example shows how this is the case. (See Table 7.2.)

TABLE 7.2.   IDENTIFY AND MANAGE THREE NEW PRODUCTS BASED ON CLASSIC CARIBBEAN AND CENTRAL AMERICAN FLAVORS

Trade-off Element	Conditions for Success

Scope
How big?
Where?
What are the benefits?
	Geography—Nationwide.
	First rollout—Florida, New England, California/Nevada
	Benefits:
	    Build brand awareness, market share among Latino households
	    Create $75M annual revenue opportunity

Time What are the major results, milestones, and the completion date?	Major results will be tracked on a monthly basis during the 12-month period. Completed by end-of-year next year.

Costs
What are the costs, and what resources will be needed?
	The budget for the initiative is $500K.
	The resources needed will be:
	    Market research—$100K
	    Production—$200K
	    Promotional budget—$100K
	    Outside agency services—$100K

The initiative looks promising, and it appears to be well thought out. But let's consider the *what ifs*. What if things change, as they always do? What if the budget has to be cut by $200,000? What if the time frame telescopes down to six months from a year because stakeholders are impatient and want to see faster results? What if senior management wants a bigger scope—more new flavors, a wider rollout, or both—with no increase in budget?

Most frequently, either the budget is cut, or the time frame shrinks. If these cuts occur, then scope must be cut as well. In managing an initiative, when one variable changes, there must be a response in the others. Initiatives can succeed only when time, scope, and money are in balance.

To Build a Road Map to Success, Think Results, Not Activities

What specific steps are necessary to carry out the initiative? If we think back to the best experience we've ever had planning an event, in hindsight it's easy to recall all the interim milestones hit to get there—the accomplishments produced along the path to a successful conclusion. There's a lesson in that insight that can be harnessed in designing a road map for carrying out initiatives.

We step into the future and place ourselves at the end of our successfully completed initiative. Then we look back to see where we've been. When we practice the Try This exercise, we see that this technique can be easily adapted for charting the course of an initiative.

TRY THIS

Work Backward

Gather Post-it notes, fine point markers, and flip chart paper. Pick a project—a fun project—say, planning a party. Pin a date on it, write it on a sticky note, and put it up on the flip chart at the far right.

Ask each participant to write down all the results that will have had to occur to make the party a success. For example, "invitations sent." Note the past tense—writing down the events as if they have already occurred helps align your brain to what you are trying to accomplish.

(Continues)

TRY THIS *(continued)*

Place the sticky notes on the flip charts, and then ask a volunteer to read them aloud. Work with the group to eliminate duplicates. Then put all notes in their proper chronological order, ending with the party.

Accountability

Once we've identified the tasks that will get us there and the order in which they must be completed, we must decide who's going to do the completing. It's as easy as *A, C, S. A* is the person who is *accountable*— the primary go-to person who is committed to delivering the result. Whoever it is owns the result. Accountability can't be assigned to others, or by others. *C* stands for *collaborators*; typically there will be more than one. *Cs* are actively involved; they are A's helping hands. In our experience, projects with collaborators have better outcomes. With collaborators, team members are not just accountable to complete the task, but also to one another. *S* stands for *stakeholders*. Who outside you and your team is affected by your completion of this result?

Table 7.3 illustrates an *accountability matrix*. It lists each result that must occur on the road to completing the initiative

TABLE 7.3.   ACCOUNTABILITY MATRIX

What	Who	When
Finalize strategies.	A = Dave C = Leslie, Tom	Draft by 3/30 Finalize 4/1
Determine priorities, trade-offs on initiatives, including criteria for decision making: current and longer term.	A = Anna C = Bill, Raul	Priorities: 6/30 Trade-offs: 5/19
Establish communication documents (audience, customers).	A = Jerry C = Chris S = Bill, internal/ Joe, external	By 4/1
Identify teams and identify what threats could be turned into opportunities. What are the "watch outs" related to leveraging our strengths?	A = Linda C = Rich, Raul S = New CIO	By 6/28

What	Who	When
Finalize the draft vision for the future that will inspire employees—how do they fit? Test it!	A = Jim C = All leadership team members S = Internal/ external PR	May–June
Make decision on international (China, e.g.)	A = John C = CFO S = Board chair	6/30
Define what structure and process changes need to be made—initial game plan only.	A = Jim C = Linda, Mike	Begin third quarter

and the date by which it must be finished. For each result, letters are assigned to identify the type of commitment each team member will have, task by task.

SMALL BUSINESS INITIATIVES

Initiatives in small businesses can be acted on quickly, but their flawless execution can be the make or break factor for the enterprise. Here's a brief study based on a composite of small firms.

Rajiv is a bilingual management consultant. His firm, Kohinoor Consulting, works with companies that have operations in the United States and on the Indian subcontinent, and with companies wanting to establish there. Kohinoor has been running workshops using its trademarked *Manage from the Middle* approach and has been educating executives from American companies on how to do business in south Asia. Rajiv hopes to grow his business by moving beyond training events to develop a series of workshop seminar products that can be marketed online.

Rajiv began in the top of the hourglass, looking at strengths, opportunities, weaknesses, and threats. His greatest strengths stemmed from his excellent relationships with top-level

(Continues)

international executives who had already been through his program. *Manage from the Middle*, Rajiv's unique approach for using mid-level managers as the catalyst for organizational change and growth, was becoming a strong brand, and of course, Rajiv himself was a strength. Looking ahead to his opportunities, he saw that many consumer package goods companies were ramping up to open factories in India. He also identified another growth opportunity by thinking in reverse— there would be a growing number of companies based in India that would be anxious to better understand how to do business in the United States.

Leveling the Peaks and Valleys

For Kohinoor, dealing with the peaks and valleys of the revenue stream was a weakness. One of the most problematic weaknesses was that clients often expected Rajiv's personal participation. He had a competent, engaged staff, but many companies insisted on having Rajiv himself lead their workshops. In the minds of consumers, Kohinoor didn't stand out—it was seen as a mix of the *Manage from the Middle* program and Rajiv himself. Rajiv also identified two major potential threats. He was concerned that a larger consulting firm might start up a business to compete with Kohinoor. He was also aware that Kohinoor could become vulnerable to an Indian-based knockoff competitor that could simply expropriate *Manage from the Middle*, change it slightly, and market it at a discount.

Rajiv identified Kohinoor's competitive advantages as the *Manage from the Middle* trademarked content, his extensive network of corporate connections developed over the years, and his multilingual, multicultural point of view and experience. His three key issues were revenue, products, and branding/positioning, and they were intertwined. How could he create a sustainable revenue stream? How could he package Kohinoor's *Manage from the Middle* training workshops for the mass market? How should he position Kohinoor, which lacked a strong distinctive identity of its own?

Transitioning to New Ventures

Taken together, the implication of these issues was that Kohinoor's dependency on event-driven and project-driven revenue, and on Rajiv as the sole personification of the company was hurting its chance to grow. There needed to be a strong effort to shift equity from Rajiv as an individual to Kohinoor Consulting. As Kohinoor makes the transition to online marketing, Rajiv will have to figure out how to sell seminars and workshops much like one would sell a consumer product. To do so, however, Kohinoor will have to defend the integrity of the *Manage from the Middle* copyright, both here and abroad. Rajiv designated three strategic priorities to address these issues: product and service development, branding and positioning, and marketing.

Accepting and Rejecting Initiatives

For each strategy, he formulated a number of initiatives:

Priority 1: Product and service development:
- Finalize development of *Manage from the Middle* 2.0
- Create suite of one-hour *Manage from the Middle* training modules that can be delivered virtually in real time

Priority 2: Branding/positioning:
- Solve branding issue for Kohinoor and *Manage from the Middle*
- Develop positioning statements for Kohinoor products and services

Priority 3: Marketing:
- Develop Kohinoor publications, using senior staff as authors/coauthors
- Create Kohinoor speaker network
- Create *Manage from the Middle* user and alumni groups online

Rajiv did reject one potentially effective initiative under Priority 1, at least for the near term. He had identified a strong

(Continues)

opportunity in a reverse market—Indian companies doing business in the United States. He actively considered opening a "second front," running workshops in India for executives wanting to have a better understanding of how to do business in the United States. Although it would have been lucrative, it would not have helped elevate his business beyond dependency on personal appearances, and the travel schedule would have been even more difficult. Once Kohinoor has launched its online products, Rajiv will take another look at running a limited number of seminars in India as a way of stimulating online sales.

EMMA'S STRATEGIES/ACTIONS

For each of her strategies, Emma put actions in place to ensure she achieves them.

Strategy: *Focus on networking with HR Executives*

- ▶ Attend 5–7 networking events per month
- ▶ Connect with 8–10 professional contacts per month

Strategy: *Conduct Informational interviews with people in target companies*

- ▶ Conduct 1 interview per week with an HR professional
- ▶ Get the names of people through LinkedIn account who are alumni of the targeted companies

Strategy: *Attend a New England school that has strong reputation for business*

- ▶ Compile listing of nearby colleges and universities offering evening and weekend classes
- ▶ Compile listing of colleges and universities that offer a complete schedule of online coursework leading to a degree
- ▶ Compare entrance requirements of potential schools with college transcript to ensure that all prerequisites have been met

Strategy: *Attend part time while working—choose an executive MBA program that meets budget needs*

▶ Compile listing of potential employers who fully or partially underwrite the cost of graduate programs for their employees
▶ Develop realistic estimate for cost of completing master's program: cost per unit, number of units, books, and other learning materials.

Strategy: *Choose an organization that has a management development program*

▶ Talk to company alumni who were recruited to other companies
▶ Benchmark their management development reputations with the other companies under consideration

Strategy: *Ensure that the hiring manager has a bias toward mentoring and people development*

▶ Schedule quarterly "check-ins" with stakeholders to assess growth
▶ Reinforce SCA skill set by refreshing proficiency in both spoken and written Arabic, particularly technical Arabic
▶ Combat shyness with assertiveness training and public speaking seminar

Chapter Summary

▶ TTW offers some simple approaches that can make a big difference in successfully moving from thinking and planning to win to acting to succeed. To start, initiatives must flow from, and be closely linked to, strategies.
▶ Setting up a team, selecting the right mix of members, and agreeing on a team charter are important success drivers. The team charter, which is specific to the initiative, contains six elements: membership, assumptions, significance/objectives, interdependencies, short- and long-term deliverables, and timing/communication.
▶ Team members should have a real voice in defining initiatives and who will have responsibility for completing them.

- When possible, initiatives are identified, and their relative merits are discussed and then ranked, using a simple scale of 1 to 3 to gauge their degree of impact: 1 = low, 2 = medium, 3 = high.
- As with ranking potential impact, the team also must assess the potential barriers and enablers to each initiative *and* develop a plan both to leverage the enablers and to reduce the barriers.
- Managing initiatives calls for keeping three factors in mind—scope, time, and costs. These triple tradeoffs are completely interdependent. Like three meshed gears, if one turns, they all turn. If one goes off kilter, they all stop.
- With initiatives in place, tasks are identified, the order in which they must be completed mapped out, and responsibilities assigned, using the *A*, *C*, and *S* model. *A* is the accountable person; *C* is the supporting collaborator, and *S* is the interested stakeholder.

Chapter 7 Exercises

How to Get Strategies Done

Mastering How to Develop and Manage Initiatives

Without initiatives and action plans, there is a high likelihood your strategies will not be fulfilled and your goals will not be met. In order to see your strategies executed, ask the following:

- How do we get this done?
- What are the most important projects, programs, or results necessary to deliver our strategies?
- Which strategy do they support?
- What specifics need to be accomplished?
- When do they have to be completed? And who are involved?

Exercise: Defining Initiatives
(Can be done at individual or group level)

Decide on initiatives:

1. Choose a strategy.
2. Identify at least three potential initiatives that are necessary to achieve the strategy.

3. Assess and rank order your initiatives against the following criteria:
   - Impact
   - Readiness
   - Capabilities
4. Choose which initiatives you are recommending to do and why.
5. Discuss with others for
   - Clarity
   - Alignment on initiatives

The deliverable is a draft of initiatives for each strategy.

Mastering TTW Team Charters

You need to create the team charter.

Exercise: Create the Team Charter

Execution of initiatives happens in teams. Select a team to design and implement the detailed work. A team charter ensures that it has explicit deliverables and a plan to accomplish the work. A team charter should answer the six categories of questions listed below.

For membership:

- Who is the sponsor (advocate)?
- Who makes up the core team?
- Who is the team leader?
- Who is the team facilitator?
- What is the transition plan for team members over the life of the initiative?

For assumptions:

- What do we assume to be true?
- What is in place that we can use?

For significance/objectives, initiative relevance, performance standards, and metrics (key performance indicators):

- What is the importance (significance) of the initiative to the business?
- What is the initiative intended to accomplish and what will signal success?
- What are the quantifiable targets of the initiative?

For interdependencies:

- ▶ Who are the stakeholders necessary for success?
- ▶ Who else do we depend on for products, ideas, and information who are not on this team?
- ▶ Who do we need to keep in the loop?
- ▶ Where is work already being done?

For deliverables:

- ▶ What do we need to deliver in the next 30, 60, or 90 days?
- ▶ What will we deliver over the next one to three years?
- ▶ What will sustain our achievements?

For timing/communication:

- ▶ What is the anticipated initiative duration?
- ▶ Communication: What is the plan and schedule for keeping the sponsors, steering committee, core team, functional managers, and other key stakeholders involved and informed?

Mastering Your Network

Exercise: Creating a Network Diagram

Now do the following as you refer to Figure 7.3:

1. Draw a circle with you/your team in the center.
2. Identify other key stakeholders.
3. Connect/draw a line between your team and other stakeholders:
   - ● 1 line—low dependency
   - ● 2 lines—moderate dependency
   - ● 3 lines—high dependency
4. Next to each stakeholder, assess the level of effectiveness between your team and the stakeholders; 1, 2, or 3 stars:
   - ● 1 star—low effectiveness
   - ● 2 stars—medium effectiveness
   - ● 3 stars—highly effective

5. Wherever you have 2 or 3 lines and only 1 or 2 stars, the initiative's progress can be blocked. Highlight these as potential barriers.
6. With the help of your table team, develop an action plan to collaborate more effectively thus reducing or eliminating the potential barriers to your initiative's success.
7. Remember to include only those actions that are within your circle of influence.

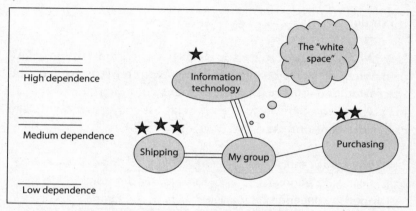

FIGURE 7.3. CHARTER ELEMENTS FOR TEAMS.

Mastering the Road Map to Completion

Exercise: Creating a Results-Based Road Map

1. "Step into the future" and pick a date by which you visualize the initiative being successfully completed.
2. Using Post-it notes—each person identifies the *results* the team needs to produce in order to deliver the initiative.
3. Group reads and removes the duplicates.
4. Sequence from left to right by asking each other:
   What result must occur first (some will happen simultaneously)?
   What happens next, and so on until all the Post-its have been sequenced?
5. Assign accountabilities for each result:
   - **Accountable.** This is the individual who owns this particular result.

- **Collaborators.** Typically two or three people actively involved in delivering the result.
- **Stakeholders.** People not actively involved in carrying out the initiative, but who have a definite interest in its success, and who may be able to play a resource procurement or other supportive role.

6. Create your visual road map. Remember to use *result language*.

Organizational Assessment

Use the following table as a checklist for identifying TTW principles and practices. This will help you to better understand where you and your team need to focus your energies. To get an idea where you believe your organization stands, read through each statement and jot down a rating:

Concept/Process	Scale: 1 = Low, 5 = High
Our organization reviews our performance against results and accountabilities on a regular basis.	
Our company has a process to ensure that every team has well-developed goals, objectives, and timelines that document the team's purpose, actions, and results.	
Project plans link to strategies and have clear accountabilities.	
Our team has a clear understanding of the criteria for the success of major initiatives.	
Our project team has a clear understanding of how to build strategic working relationships to enable collaboration.	

Review individual items. Look for items where you scored lower (3 and below) and think about the following questions:

- ▶ What do I believe is driving the score?
- ▶ What do I need to stop, start, or continue doing?
- ▶ What do I hope the result to be?

Bringing Everything Together: From Thinking to Acting to Winning

How do you get ahead? How do you win? From 1981 through 1995, every one of General Electric's more than 100,000 employees knew exactly how to do it: Make sure your product or business held the number one or two position in its market. If it did, you won. You were helping make GE the most competitive global enterprise in the world. If not, you lost. Your product or business got sold or shut down.

That was Jack Welch's vision for General Electric when he was CEO and transformed the company from a lethargic, underperforming aggregation of dissimilar parts into a dynamic, cohesive, purpose-oriented global icon. Jack Welsh knew that powerfully communicating to every corner of his vast worldwide organization was a make or break factor. And he knew he had to start with something that was both simple and basic. He had to start with a statement that answered the question: How did GE intend to win with its businesses?

It had to be clear and easily understood, and it had to come to life and guide all employees every day they came to work. And the GE vision did just that in unaltered form for nearly 15 years with one simple statement: GE would be the most competitive enterprise in the world by being number one or two in every market—by fixing underperforming businesses or selling or closing them if they couldn't be upgraded to a top rank.

Communication brings everything together. Once we've gone through the entire TTW process and once we've completed our top to bottom hourglass venture, the critical part of the journey begins—transforming thinking and plans into actions and accomplishments. As Lee Iacocca, the former chairman of Chrysler, once said: "You can have brilliant ideas, but if you don't get them across, your ideas won't get you anywhere."

The best-laid plans are worthless unless they're communicated and understood. And not by just a select few, but by everyone. This means that they must be communicated with a loud volume and with great frequency and repetition.

Key Messages Frame Everything

Let's see where the communications process begins. It starts with key messages that frame everything we've done. The three elements in each message answer three basic questions: What's going on? What are we going to do? What will be the result? Or, said another way, each key message must contain the situation, action, and impact so understanding is both quick and certain.

It's important to underscore the elements that make a best-in-class key message. Obviously, since we are communicating—attempting to gain the attention, awareness, and understanding of another person, team, large group, or total organization—our message must be compelling. It must hook our intended audience. All too often, we find key messages couched in grandiose language that have a high-sounding tone to them but that don't communicate.

Without a sense of urgency, messages usually don't break through and register. In today's world where we confront such an information overload at home, at work, and even in what used to be our leisure time, messages must grab our interest. Take a situation statement (element 1 of key messages) that says: We're in third place in the widget market. We want to get to second place.

That sounds like a nice thing to do, but what does it mean to me? And why should it go to the top of my list and become a priority item? But when the sense of urgency and relevance are present, the impact is real and the priority is likely to be very high as in the following phrasing of the situation: We're in third place in the widget market. If we don't get to second place, our business will be shut down and our jobs will be lost. We need action now by all of us.

So a sense of urgency is important to convey. But if we're trying also to get action (element 2 of key messages), then we also have to be specific and concrete. Again, a statement that is filled with high-sounding generalizations won't get people lined up to act: As we start our march to number two in widgets, we must be bold in our thinking, fierce in our assault, and persistent in our follow-through until our goal is achieved.

But phrasing that is concrete and ties back to our SWOT will provide understanding and also be a confidence builder that will generate action: We will enter new niche markets by using our strength in widget design, and we'll strengthen our customer service by improving our already strong just-in-time delivery performance.

By providing specifics that relate back to our SWOT and by focusing on a vital few initiatives rather than a rambling laundry list, we create a sense that our mission is very possible.

Since our key messages also provide a sense of the impact of our action (element 3 is what the result will be), the scope of the outcome is important. In our widget illustration, widgets are just one of 25 divisions of the Global Manufacturing Corp. Elevating the widget division to second place will be very meaningful at a divisional level, but is not likely to move the share price of Global. Defining the right scope is important in each of the three elements of key messages.

Situation, Action, Impact

Let's now look at a few illustrations of some key messages that we think do an excellent job of communicating: A small northeastern chain of upscale supermarkets found its sales slipping as market dynamics changed. Here are key messages:

> **Situation.** Our upscale positioning is losing its appeal as consumers are demanding local sourcing of nutritious, organic food for themselves and their children. Our continued existence rests on our ability to change our positioning and meet our consumers' needs.

> **Action.** We will increase our organic locally sourced produce, meat, fish, and other fresh items by 50 percent, which we will highlight in a new marketing campaign. We also will conduct workshops and in-store information and education activities for our shoppers.

> **Impact.** Our projections call for a sales increase of 5 percent in year one and 4 percent in each of the following two years.

A company that specialized in direct selling of home goods faced sharply declining sales as a result of the recession and competition from new discount-priced retailers:.

> **Situation.** Our declining sales and profits present a serious threat to our company. Because of the economic slowdown, our customers are looking for low prices and are migrating to discount retailers and online sellers. Our marketing and product development groups don't have the relevant knowledge and aren't working closely enough with our sales representatives to address the issues.

> **Action.** We will bring our marketing and sales groups together to close the knowledge gaps and strengthen our product development efforts. We will build a product portfolio that addresses our customers' needs in the economic downturn. And we will create a strong e-commerce sales presence.

▶ **Impact.** Our revenues will increase by 12 percent in three years by expanding our consumer base, improving our product portfolio, and increasing the engagement level of our sales representatives.

Research showed a fashion accessories company that its previously cutting-edge designs were losing their market appeal:

▶ **Situation.** Our accessories are being attacked by a hot competitor. Our current product development process must be updated so we can maintain our "first-in-the-market" leadership position. Otherwise we are in danger of losing our "cool factor."

▶ **Action.** Our product development process will be overhauled, and new marketing concepts, covering PR, new media, and product placement, will be created. We will invest disproportionately in high-growth, developing markets such as China and Brazil.

▶ **Impact.** Our accessories will regain their leadership based on our speed to market with innovative products. Strong growth in large developing markets will help propel sales growth of 15 percent in two years.

Showing the Pieces as One

With the key messages as a guide, we can now move to something we call *plan-on-a-page* that gives a bird's-eye view of all elements of TTW from visions and goals to strategies and initiatives. The plan-on-a-page fosters alignment and encourages collaboration since it shows the interrelatedness of the different pieces that make up the whole.

As we can see from Figure 8.1, the plan-on-a-page does just what it says. It lays out a full annual operating plan complete with the vision and goals that are guiding it, the strategies that propel it, and the specific initiatives that will achieve them. Presenting the plan in this format makes it very understandable to a team, unit, or organization. A common problem and complaint within companies is that one function has no idea what another function is doing or how the two functions should relate to each other. With plan-on-a-page, *all* the *initiatives* are shown, and the linkages are evident.

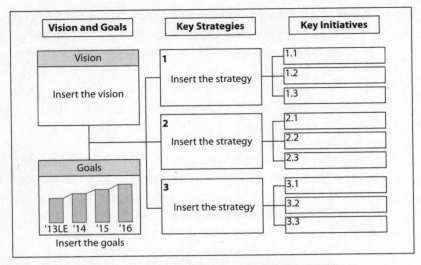

FIGURE 8.1. STRATEGIC GROWTH: PLAN-ON-A-PAGE.

Gaining alignment is much easier when all the elements are clearly laid out and easy to grasp. And the plan-on-a-page breathes life into a document that often is barely acknowledged except in mandatory reviews and almost never referenced for guidance. It underscores the importance of a plan being a living document, not a static oversized binder or spreadsheet. The exercise section at the end of this chapter has activities that show how to use the plan-on-a-page.

Making Visions Come Alive

Effective communication must be all inclusive. So let's look at what's important at different levels. At the broadest level, we must gain everyone's understanding of the vision we developed in the top of the hourglass. Visions are not just an important part of the TTW process to generate our initiatives and action plans; they also are a critical factor in communicating and executing action.

As we saw in Chapter 5, visions aren't just nice words and platitudes. They must be unique, engaging, compelling, and concise. They must be so memorable and so accessible that all associates throughout a company, regardless of their title and level, will know and can effortlessly describe what the vision is, what it means, and how it relates to their individual jobs.

As Jack Welsh says in his book *Winning* (New York: HarperCollins, 2005), leaders have to "make visions come alive by being certain they contain no jargon, no noble but vague goals and no targets that are so blurry they can't be met." The leader's direction, he says, "has to be so vivid that if you randomly woke up one of your employees in the middle of the night and asked him, Where are you going? he could still answer in a half-sleep stupor, 'We're going to keep improving our service to individual contractors and expand our market by aggressively reaching out to small wholesalers.'"

As Dave Moran of Keurig Green Mountain noted (see Chapter 5), "The clearer the statement [vision] is, the simpler it is, the more compelling it is, and the more memorable and more inspiring it will be." And Keurig's vision captures all those qualities: A brewer on every countertop, a beverage for every occasion.

Again, from Dave Moran: "One of the key things that has driven our success is the tremendous clarity around our vision of how we would approach growth. We boiled it down to one sentence that everybody could remember. And then we made sure it was understood by all. Everyone . . . knows that sentence and knows exactly what we are trying to achieve."

Doug Conant, the retired CEO of the Campbell Soup Company, goes even further in describing the importance of projecting messages and communicating at all times. In his book *TouchPoints: Creating Powerful Leadership Connections in the Smallest of Moments* (San Francisco: Jossey-Bass, 2011), which he coauthored with leadership expert Mette Norgaard, Doug describes a typical situation in which a leader, trying to finish a proposal that is critical to his department's future, is interrupted by a knock on the door from a team member who needs help with a problem. Doug asks: How do you respond? With irritation and a brush-off or by stopping and helping?

"As a leader, you make those choices all day, every day. The 'knock on the door' happens over and over again . . . all with questions to answer, concerns to address, problems to solve and fires to put out. Some days it feels as though the information age has morphed into the interruption age." But if you step back and look at all these interruptions with a different perspective, each one could be a relationship-building, communications moment.

"Each of the many connections you make . . . is an opportunity to establish high performance expectations, to infuse the agenda with greater clarity and more energy, and to influence the course of events," says Doug, who is now chairman of Avon Products, the Kellogg Executive Leadership Institute (KELI) at Northwestern University, and Conant Leadership. "Each is a chance to transform an ordinary moment into a TouchPoint." And Doug's track record at Campbell's, where he reversed a precipitous decline in market value and employee engagement, is evidence of the power of this practice.

Throughout his career, Jim Kilts, who headed Kraft, Nabisco, and Gillette, had a very straightforward vision: "Build total brand value by innovating to deliver consumer value and customer leadership faster, better, and more completely than our competitors." That's a simple statement, but Jim made countless speeches, presentations, videos, and town hall talks and held informal coffees to explain the meaning and intended impact of each concept and phrase. The vision became very real and immediate.

Aligning Compensation with Vision

Regardless of their clarity and everyone's understanding, visions won't succeed unless compensation is aligned with them. Again, Jack Welsh notes that if you want people to live and breathe the vision, you must show them the money—with salary, bonus, and significant special financial rewards. "Vision is an essential element of the leader's job. But no vision is worth the paper it's printed on unless it is communicated constantly and reinforced with rewards. Only then will it leap off the page—and come to life." And by "leader," we mean leaders at all levels within any organization. If we want to win, we have to communicate our visions.

Projecting Messages Through Every Channel

Communication isn't just about e-mails, video speeches, and PowerPoint presentations. It must be infused within every aspect of an organization's day-to-day activities. Messages must be projected and reinforced through every channel and in every mode that's available.

As Harvard Business School Professor John P. Kotter says, key messages and visions must be worked into a leader's hour-by-hour activities. They must be part of a discussion about a business problem by describing how solutions fit into a bigger picture. In a performance appraisal, an associate should know how her behavior helps or hurts the vision. A quarterly review shouldn't just talk about numbers; it should describe how the division's actions are contributing to the key messages. Even simple question-and-answer sessions should have answers that tie back to the vision. In short, Professor Kotter says that all existing communication channels should be used to broadcast the vision. Even management education courses should be replaced with courses that focus on the vision. "The guiding principle is simple: use every possible channel, especially those that are being wasted on nonessential information." ("Leading Change: Why Transformation Efforts Fail," *Harvard Business Review*, January 2007).

Kotter's description of the steps and elements essential to transforming a company apply to our concepts about excellence in communications and the entire TTW process. He describes eight stages. The first involves establishing a sense of urgency that discusses crises and potential crises as well as opportunities. Then comes forming a powerful guiding coalition, which means assembling a group of people who will assist with the communication—people who also have enough power to lead change around the vision.

The next two steps involve defining a clear vision and developing the all-out communications strategies to get it known and understood. For the communication to enable action, obstacles to change also have to be eliminated by changing the systems and structure that undermine the vision and short-term wins that show the vision's potential must be underscored. As the process continues, more improvements and changes will be implemented and communicated. And finally, linkages between new behaviors and the vision are communicated to help anchor the vision. (Our next chapter is all about the anchoring change concept, so we discuss it there in detail.) Also, take a look at the material quoted below in which Professor Kotter outlines the pitfalls of his process. They have a direct relevance to our TTW process.

BEWARE THE PITFALLS

For each of the stages in the process, there is a corresponding pitfall.

1. **Not establishing a great enough sense of urgency.** Half of all change efforts fail at the start. When is the urgency rate high enough? When 75% of management is genuinely convinced that the status quo is, in the words of the CEO of a European company, "more dangerous than launching into the unknown."

2. **Not creating a powerful enough guiding coalition.** In successful transformation efforts, the chairman or president or general manager of the division, plus another 5 to 50 others—including many, but not all, of the most influential people in the unit—develop a shared commitment to renewal [the vision].

3. **Lacking a vision.** Without a coherent and sensible vision, a change effort dissolves into a list of confusing and incompatible projects. If you can't communicate the vision in five minutes or less and get a reaction that indicates understanding and interest, your work in this stage isn't done.

4. **Undercommunicating the vision by a factor of ten.** Use every existing communications vehicle to get the vision out. Incorporate the vision into routine discussions about business problems.

5. **Not removing obstacles to the new vision.** Renewal requires the removal of obstacles—systemic or human—to the vision. One company's transformation ground to a halt

because the executive in charge of the largest division didn't change his own behavior, didn't reward the unconventional ideas called for in the vision, and left the human resource systems intact even though they were incompatible with the new ideals.

6. **Not systemically planning for and creating short-term wins.** Clearly recognizable victories within the first year or two of a change effort help convince doubters that the change effort is going to be worth all the trouble.

7. **Declaring victory too soon.** At this stage, it is fine to celebrate a short-term win, but it's catastrophic to declare the war is over.

8. **Not anchoring changes in the corporation's culture.** If they are to stick, new behaviors must be rooted in the social norms and shared values of a corporation. To accomplish this, make a conscious attempt to show people that the new behaviors and approaches have improved performance. Also make sure that the next generation of top management embodies the new approach.

(Excerpted from John P. Kotter, "Leading Change: Why Transformation Efforts Fail," *Harvard Business Review*, HBR OnPoint 2000.)

Communicating Management Style

Former Gillette CEO Jim Kilts took his efforts to communicate about his expectations, his accessibility, his style of management, and even his idiosyncrasies to another level. Within a matter of days of assuming a new position, Jim would distribute a simply worded, bullet-pointed message that covered dozens of issues and topics—everything from the importance of integrity (Do what is right and you'll never go wrong. Integrity is the starting point for all business decisions.) to how to behave at staff meetings (Pay attention: no sidebar conversations or secondary tasks. When talking, stick to the subject.) This full document, which is very instructive, appears at the end of the chapter.

Leading Memorably from the Front

"I believe communication is a critical element in changing culture and behavior," says former Procter & Gamble vice chairman Ed Shirley. "I learned very early the importance of being out there, leading from the front and communicating the message. If the leader isn't a good communicator, no one knows where they are going. The Think to Win framework allowed me to communicate in a systematic way. It's ingrained in how I think, and how I lead."

Ed used the TTW process to develop a clear and forthright appraisal of the situation he found when he joined P&G from Gillette. "Coming in as an outsider, I looked at things through a different lens. Even so, I was able to quickly gain people's trust. The first thing I did was to prepare a very transparent situation assessment. It was thorough and comprehensive, and I communicated it in a straightforward manner, so we could let the facts drive our decision making."

Getting everyone aligned on the situation assessment allowed Ed to put forth his recommendations. "I was very clear, especially with the board," he says. "I framed the situation analysis as reality, and our plans as hope. 'Here is how I see things,' I said. 'Here is our reality; here is what we're going to do about it—the choices we are making, and this is why I believe it's going to work.'"

He also used an imaginative device to communicate with his board. To reinforce the concept of looking at the international sales of P&G's personal care products from the consumers' perspectives, Ed brought in two cutout figures, one male, one female, as props for his presentation. He then pointed out which body parts were being overlooked in major markets around the globe.

"For men, in most parts of the world, we are capturing the face and beard only. For the rest of him, we have zero," he explained. "We are not winning in many of these markets because we are not addressing enough body parts. We are not meeting a woman's deodorant needs in Brazil, nor her moisturizer needs in India. If the consumer really was the boss, we'd be meeting more of her needs."

Ed's key messages were rooted in TTW, and he found a memorable way of communicating them to the board. It was the beginning of a new companywide effort to market to the "complete man" and "complete woman" in several key developing markets.

Building Blocks of Execution

Communication is fundamental to the process that propels execution. Within a company, execution starts with the annual plan that defines goals for the year. But the building blocks are critical to their attainment, and communication is critical to each of the blocks.

Let's look at some of the frequently used building blocks. Often these will involve weekly postings that relate both accomplishments and issues or difficulties. These postings are shared widely among all functions, divisions, and units within the company so that awareness is high about what's happening. Since no unit or function operates independently of others, this sharing is essential to ensure a connectedness and alignment as initiatives move forward or midcourse corrections occur.

All too often the separate silos created by a lack of communication are the reason execution stumbles. Weekly postings provide a base level of communication that will be complemented with meetings and other communications.

These postings are accompanied by weekly meetings that set the agenda for the following week and, again, ensure alignment for all the participants. The meetings should be kept short. They aren't a time for grandstanding or pontificating. They should provide dialogue on what happened last week, what went right, what went wrong, what's being done to address issues, and what's planned for the week ahead.

Beyond the weekly activities, there are quarterly priorities with quarterly meetings to track progress, identify issues, and make necessary adjustments or corrections. The quarterly priorities provide an opportunity for rating performance so all team members know how they are doing and what parts of their game have to be improved.

The quarterly priorities tie directly to the annual plan, which provides the basis for the key messages. The entire approach represents constant communication—a continuous loop that yields clarity and alignment.

That's how communication brings everything together. It's one very important element in transforming thinking and plans into actions and accomplishments.

Chapter Summary

▶ Once we've completed our top to bottom hourglass venture, the critical part of the journey begins—transforming thinking and plans into actions and accomplishments.

▶ Key messages frame everything. The three elements in each message answer three basic questions: What's going on? What are we going to do? What will be the results? Each key message must contain situation, action, and impact so understanding is both quick and certain.

▶ Plan-on-a-page gives a bird's-eye view of all elements of TTW from visions and goals to strategies and initiatives. Plan-on-a-page fosters alignment and encourages collaboration since it shows the interrelatedness of the different pieces that make up the whole.

▶ Visions are a critical factor in communicating and executing. They aren't just nice words and platitudes. They must be unique, engaging, compelling, concise, and memorable. Everyone must know what the vision means and how it relates to their individual job.

▶ Execution starts with the annual plan that defines goals for the year. But weekly and quarterly building blocks are critical to their attainment, and communication is critical to each of the blocks.

The following is excerpted from *Doing What Matters* by James M. Kilts, John F. Manfredi, and Robert L. Lorber (New York: Crown, 2007).

The Real Deal—A Complete List of Horrors

I started my . . . presentation [to the Gillette leadership team] by review-ing the conclusions distilled from my weeks of research, discussions, and trade contacts. I told them that the Gillette Board of Directors would be given the same presentation. So everyone would know they would be hearing the real deal, not something specially crafted for this initial meeting.

I started by talking about Gillette's formidable strengths—iconic brands, high growth, high margin product categories, unmatched technology and product innovation and a great global presence. The group nodded their assent. As I went through the weaknesses—flat sales and earnings, consistently missed profit targets, declining market shares, decreasing ad spending, increasing overheads, soaring capital expenditures, and across the board weak financial metrics—I could sense both unease and defensiveness.

Always Confront Reality

Throughout the discussion, my message was that we would confront reality. There would be no more top-down dictums; no more setting of targets that couldn't be made; or making of promises that couldn't be kept. Outstanding performance would be expected from everyone, but we would be working against reality-based, achievable objectives.

We would cut no corners; integrity mattered big time, across the board—morally, ethically, and legally. In all, this day 1 session gave my new senior management team a total immersion in my views on managing, business, and people. Let me go over some of the areas covered:

My style might be described as follows:

▶ Open; straightforward; what you see, is what you get. I play no games and have no hidden agendas. I say what I mean; there is nothing to read between the lines.

▶ Action oriented—fair, but somewhat impatient. I value action and accomplishment; I dislike rationalizations and excuses.

▶ Want no surprises. If the sky is falling, tell me. I don't want to learn about it by reading a newspaper.

I use no gotchas, games, or tricks.

▶ Will avoid "gotchas." No games; no tricks. I judge people based on performance.

▶ If something bothers you, I want open dialogue. I am not a mind reader. Let me know if you think something is wrong.

▶ Expect excellence, reward the same. I am demanding, but I reward excellent performance—probably at a level that will surprise you.

▶ Like and accept challenges. I spent my life building brands and running consumer businesses. My greatest satisfaction comes from dealing with tough issues.

► Save a tree. Avoid memos, if you can. When you can't, keep them short.

► Ask my advice early. I've had more than 25 years of experience. Give me a chance, and I probably can help you.

► Often wrong, never uncertain. I never equivocate. I make quick decisions. So when I'm wrong, let me know . . . quickly.

My Management Philosophy

► It's all about building total brand value
   ● Superior marketing driven by consumer and customer understanding
   ● Competitively advantaged products and cost structures

► Believe cost and quality are compatible. I want lowest costs, but insist on no compromise of quality.

► Strongly believe in keeping things simple:
   ● Organization structures
   ● Communications
   ● Process
   ● Priorities

► Clear and full accountabilities. Believe in matrixed organization. Organizational matrices facilitate performance, but individual responsibility is essential, which means that one person must be accountable for ultimate results.

Never Over Promise; Always Over Deliver

► A promise made is a promise kept. Never over promise; always over deliver. I've lived by these words throughout my entire career.

► Believe in alignment and linkage—operating managers working together with strong staff input make the best decisions. The 8 to 10 days spent at quarterly offsites, plus weekly staff meetings, plus weekly reports are all designed to reinforce and assure linkage and alignment.

► My key function is to set direction, allocate resources, and provide support. Your key responsibility is to get the results agreed upon in objectives and priorities. I want it to be clear that my managers have a lot of autonomy to act and complete accountability to achieve.

Level the Silos, Increase the Sharing

▶ The more communication, cooperation, and support, the farther and faster we will go. If sharing is increased, silos leveled, and alignment improved, great results will follow.

▶ Innovation must be applied in all aspects of business; innovation must define how we think and act.

Good Ideas Are Easy to Come By

▶ Good ideas, well executed, make the difference. The two elements must come together in order to be meaningful. Good ideas are easy to come by; they're meaningless unless they are well executed.

▶ Finally, although not really part of my management philosophy, I feel so strongly about it that I include it: I hate anyone saying: "Jim said" or "Jim wants," or "the board said" or "the board wants" as the reason for doing, or not doing, something. Things are done, or not done, based on rigorous assessments and considered deliberations. I have experienced firsthand how disruptive and demoralizing top-down dictums can be, especially when no explanation accompanies them.

My Expectations of You:

▶ Outstanding performance. Promises must be kept: we make our numbers; we do what we say we will do. This is another precept that underscores the need for excellence and accountability.

▶ Support decisions once made; contribute before decisions are made. Nothing is worse than someone who sits silently during a decision-making process and then, after the fact, seeks to undercut the action. I don't tolerate efforts that subvert.

▶ Help each other work out problems. Sometimes it's pride, or fear of losing authority and standing, but peers are often reluctant to seek help from each other, even though they all are part of the same team. I do everything I can to break down that attitude.

Untangling Tough Issues—Think Back to Parents and Teachers

▶ Integrity—moral, ethical, legal. Integrity is the starting point for all business decisions. I always say that you can resolve the most difficult and entangled issue if you just "do the right thing."

Always be guided by the law. But also think back to what your parents, teachers, minister, priest or rabbi told you. Do what's right and you'll never go wrong.

▶ Be leaders of your business, function, and your people. Upgrade your organization continually. Since I wanted Gillette to be the best consumer products company in the world, I needed a team of top performers—leaders who would be the best at running their business units or functions and in managing and developing their people. Continual dissatisfaction must characterize the leader, which results in continual improvement and upgrading throughout his or her operation.

No Room for Leakers

▶ Appropriate confidentiality—both internally and externally. Gillette was one of the most porous companies I had ever encountered. I was not used to leaks, which often signal low morale and a disenchanted workforce. While I intended to work on the root causes, I wanted everyone to know that "leakers" would not be tolerated.

▶ Don't want competition among functions, or the senior staff. Anything that even hints at it is counterproductive. If the top people in the company are sniping at each other, or appear to be, the impact is corrosive throughout.

Don't Make Smart Mistakes Twice

▶ My policy on mistakes:
  - You . . . don't make dumb mistakes
  - I . . . don't punish smart mistakes
  - You . . . don't make smart mistakes twice
  - An omission mistake is just as bad, or worse, than a commission mistake.

▶ I do not want a risk-averse organization. But I also won't tolerate slipshod preparation and thinking that lead to failures. When the right process and thinking do not succeed, that's fine, but learn from failure. Whatever you do, never say: "I'm not to blame because I didn't know that X, Y, or Z would happen." You should have known, believe me.

▶ Appropriate discipline and fact-based analytics must be used in assessing businesses, infrastructures, and growth opportunities. The more facts that you have and the better analysis that you can do, the more likely you'll make the right decision.

Great Freedom, but Not Complete Autonomy

▶ You should involve me in major strategic and operational decisions. I give my managers great freedom to act, but not complete autonomy. I must be fully consulted and engaged in all major decisions.

▶ I need enough information and insights, not just data, so I can understand what's happening and why. (One of my first actions at Gillette was to discontinue a series of monthly reports that resulted in several thick binders of data that provided no real insight or understanding about what was happening in the business, or why.) Quality, not quantity matters.

Weekly Staff Meetings:

▶ Why weekly meetings?
- Want firsthand update on the business
- Business conditions warrant it
- Helps assure alignment
- Share what's going on so you can do your job and gain full executive communication.

Resistance Precedes Experience

▶ Resistance to weekly staff meetings almost always precedes experiencing them. Concerns about the time spent is always overcome by the understanding and insight received about other parts of the business, and also about the impact on the individual's own unit.

▶ Attendance required; on time; no substitution without prior Jim Kilts's approval. I want the point understood that I take the weekly meetings seriously, and so should everyone else.

▶ Weekly, Monday, 10 a.m. to 12 noon; can be extended, as needed.

▶ Agenda
- Suggest items and requested time needed to CFO by Wednesday preceding meeting; indicate if significant action/decision desired at meeting
- Agenda reviewed by Jim Kilts and issued by Thursday

Weekly staff meetings provide an opportunity for full executive team review and decision on an issue in a timely fashion; no waiting for monthly or quarterly session.

▶ Confidentiality
- No gossip
- Reinforce with your assistants and others

(By underscoring the importance of confidentiality, we had virtually no issues. In fact, a group of about a half dozen top senior executives managed to keep Gillette's merger talks with Procter & Gamble confidential for several months, a remarkable achievement.)

Always Consensus, Often Unanimous

▶ Decision process
- Consensus—all views heard.
- Final decisions by Jim Kilts, as needed.

In my five years at Gillette, we always reached consensus on key decisions—often with unanimity. There was no time that I recall having to override a decision made by the team.

▶ Behavior
- Pay attention: No sidebar conversations or secondary tasks; really listen
- Stick to subject
- Openness
- Prework: Preparation when needed
- Jokes, fun are okay

Discipline, focus and engagement are things I expect from all people at all times, and weekly staff meetings are no exception. However, I realize that fun, jokes, and humor are often the best way to create bonds and bring the group together.

Minimizing Grandstanding

▶ Once around the table process
- Limited to three minutes each
- Items requiring more time to be on agenda

I like to give everyone an opportunity to be heard; the three-minute limit keeps things focused and keeps anyone from grandstanding.

Other Housekeeping

▶ One-on-ones; your call. Since I manage by walking around, I drop in on my direct reports, and many others, plus have lots of telephone conversations. However, I do not have regularly scheduled one-on-ones with my direct reports other than our quarterly review of priorities. If anyone feels the need, I welcome them.

▶ Only your administrative assistant sets meetings with me through my administrative assistant. A process for scheduling meetings helps keep control of what easily can become a chaotic calendar.

Impress with Accomplishments, Not with Number of Meetings and Memos

▶ Less is more
- Meetings, paper, attendees

Some managers believe they impress you with the number of memos and plans they send and meetings they schedule. I want to make sure that weekly staff meetings serve their purpose, which is to limit the need for interim communications, meetings, etc.

▶ No such thing as a "casual meeting" with outside stakeholders such as investment analysts, bankers, shareholders, etc. Most senior managers know how risky meetings, even supposedly off-the-record meetings, can be with outsiders who easily can misinterpret and misuse the information provided. I believe in having specialists deal with specialists.

Chapter 8 Exercises

Mastering Communication

Communication means much more than providing information. The message must be easily understood and compelling to ensure both interest and retention. When delivering your message, concise is best. TTW provides two powerful tools; each of which distills your message down to a single page.

Mastering the Key Message Template

Key messages are very important. They focus the audience with a brief and compelling statement that is both easy to understand and easy to recall. Our key message template helps you structure the answer to the question, How do we communicate succinctly? A key message has three basic components:

- ▶ **Situation:** What is going on?
- ▶ **Action:** How are we going to address it?
- ▶ **Impact:** What will the result be?

Exercise: Creating Your Key Message

1. Review the content of your work
2. Create three to four bullet points for each of the following components:
   a. **Situation:** What is going on—summarizes what you know. *Think:* Top half of the hourglass— seven Cs analysis drilled down through the key issues and implications—what is the most important issue?
   b. **Action:** What to do about it—summarizes your intent. *Think:* Strategies
   c. **Impact:** What you're aiming to get out of it—what will the result be? *Think*: Goals and measures (3Ms)
3. Consolidate on one page:
   a. Review for clarity
   b. Discuss for additions/changes
   c. Align on key messages

The deliverable is a key message page. The purpose is to summarize and map out the issue being solved in a very simple manner that is easy to understand.

Typically, key messages have three to four bullets points for each area. Key messages look backward—they need to be completed at the end of the TTW process. You should be able to quickly and clearly tell anyone the essentials of what you've been working on. If you have trouble formulating your key message, it may be a sign to go back to make sure you've not left out any steps.

Mastering Plan-on-a-Page

The plan-on-a-page, as shown previously, is a visual road map that serves as a catalyst for communication. On a single piece of paper or computer screen, it answers the question, How will we win? The plan-on-a-page makes the line of sight clear; from your analysis of facts on the ground, to goals and objectives for the future, to strategic priorities and programs and initiatives to deliver them.

Begin with your key messages. Map each element against the plan-on-a-page template. Each element and detail should connect with the next. Hone your presentation down to the fewest possible words to summarize each segment in the clearest, most succinct manner.

Exercise: Creating Your Plan-on-a-Page

1. Review the contents of your work
2. Consolidate on one page:
   a. Review for clarity
   b. Discuss for additions/changes
   c. Finalize the plan-on-a-page

Refer back to Figure 8.1 shown earlier in this chapter.

Organizational Assessment

Use the following table as a checklist for identifying TTW principles and practices. This will help you to better understand where you and your team need to focus your energies. To get an idea of where you believe your organization stands, read through each statement and jot down a rating:

Concept/Process	Scale: 1= Low, 5 = high
When asked, we can easily articulate our situational assessment, recommendations, and impact to others.	
We deploy questions in a logical manner as a mechanism for identifying issues and determining solutions.	
Our company has processes to ensure that there is ongoing, two-way communication and sharing of information.	
Communication about goals, strategies, and initiatives is simple to understand and visible on one page.	
We use formal communication tools to communicate currently reality and the choices the organization will have to make to win in the marketplace.	

Review individual items. Look for items where you scored lower (3 and below) and think about the following questions:

- ▶ What do I believe is driving the score?
- ▶ What do I need to stop, start, or continue doing?
- ▶ What do I hope the result to be?

The Winning Never Ends: Anchoring Change

When legendary Coach Geno Auriemma's UConn women's basketball team won its first national NCAA title, why was he so confident many more would follow? And what did Coach Anson Dorrance know that led him to believe he could create a dynasty of winning women's soccer teams at the University of North Carolina?

Both coaches had put mechanisms in place to ensure lasting success, not just for a particular team in a particular year, but year after year after year. Both coaches institutionalized systematic ways to mold and educate their players, physically and mentally. They established schedules that extended far beyond the playing season. They had a 12-month calendar of activities for team members, including practice routines, assessment tools, leadership seminars, a schedule of meetings, and off-season events.

For Dorrance and Auriemma, their career won-lost records and championship banners speak for themselves. The changes they initiated when they joined the teams, together with the adjustments and refinements they made over time, transformed how their sports are run. Their systems became the anchors for a new way of doing things: change, winning, and sustainability come together as an enduring concept.

The coaches also became talent magnets. Recruitment became easier as star players gravitated to them. And each new generation was shaped by the systems already in place. "The teams changed composition as players turned over, but the structures and processes remained," writes Harvard Business School professor Rosabeth Moss Kanter, a leading voice on change over the last 25 years. "The winning teams that resulted were not a force of nature; they were a product of professional disciplines and structures." She emphasizes the importance of formally implanting these mechanisms into the institution. "The architecture of change involves the design and construction of new patterns, or the reconceptualization of old ones, to make new, and hopefully more productive, actions." (*Confidence: How Winning Streaks and Losing Streaks Begin and End,* Rosabeth Moss Kanter, New York: Crown, 2004)

These disciplines and structures are at least as important as the individuals who install them. Kanter points out that "Nelson Mandela's leadership in South Africa gained its power not just through his inspiring message, but through the structure of a new government, legislation, and, importantly, formal events such as town meetings on a new constitution, and hearings by the Truth and Reconciliation Commission."

Kanter highlights the essential role of leadership: "Leaders embed the winners' behavior in the culture, not just through person-to-person and generation-to-generation transfers of norms, but also through the formal mechanisms that embed positive behavior in team and organizational routines."

Imagine the energy, efficiency, and creativity of an organization where everyone thinks to win. Our process alters the way

THE WINNING NEVER ENDS: ANCHORING CHANGE

people think, plan, and act. But TTW doesn't end with execution. Long-term success calls for the same systematic change Professor Kanter describes. It requires embedding changes in the culture to sustain and anchor winning results. As we proceed, we detail several proven approaches to achieve this end.

Let's start with how the skilled use of symbols and signals can help to anchor changes. Often the visual reminders of a symbol can reinforce concepts even more powerfully than words.

A Recipe for Change

Change is anchored into the organization when leaders are deliberate about how they use symbols and rituals to drive action and behavior. Strong leaders who want to create change and ensure that it sticks are deliberate in how they plan, act, and serve as role models for TTW behavior. In their bestseller *Leadership Sustainability*, Norm Smallwood and Dave Ulrich (New York: McGraw-Hill, 2013) emphasize the role leaders play in anchoring change by the attention they pay to the signals and symbols of their actions.

Jim Holbrook put symbols to work when he assumed leadership at the cereal division of Post Foods. Jim knew that he and his team had to act quickly to put in place a turnaround plan to address both short- and long-term business issues. If done correctly, it would provide the blueprint for the future.

Jim and his senior management embraced the key principles of TTW. They created a growth plan that they branded the *recipe*. It had all the elements of the TTW process—good internal/external assessment, clear goals, strategic priorities, and initiatives. Understanding of the external landscape as well as internal strengths were identified as *ingredients* for success. Jim has made *recipe* and *cooking* the metaphors and symbols for how the leadership team drives execution through the organization. All Post functions and business units create their own recipes, which drive alignment throughout the organization. The symbolic recipes exist today as living, breathing documents. The *recipe-on-a-page* is displayed throughout Post headquarters. And the business is responding with solid sales growth in a category that's declining.

GLOBAL TURNAROUND—GLOBAL ANCHORING

Gillette was in free fall. The company that once was the bellwether and standard setter for the consumer products sector had not only lost its luster, but it had lost its way.

Gillette was still dominant in its core shaving business—in the United States and around the world. Innovations seemed to be no problem. New shaving systems that traded up users from one premium level to another were in high gear. Competition was both muted and fragmented. No rival really existed at a global level. So what was the problem? What was driving Gillette stock down day after day, quarter after quarter?

There were lots of theories and hundreds of suggestions for how to set things on the right course. But the basic problem was simple. Gillette lacked an important core competence. It lacked strategic thinking. And the lack was profound, widespread, and reached all levels of the organization. It affected all its divisions and locations around the world. No area of the company was untouched by this critical absence.

The strategic thinking process that should have been guiding this global powerhouse was on hiatus, which is why bringing strategic thinking to Gillette ranked so high as a priority when Jim Kilts took over as the new CEO. The board had recruited Jim for his individual track record as a master of turning around troubled iconic consumer products companies and divisions. He had done it many times during his 25-year tenure with General Foods, Oscar Mayer, Kraft, and Nabisco with exceptional results.

So the Gillette board members knew that Kilts was an individual winner. But they also knew that he won by surrounding himself with bright, talented people who knew how to think strategically and then act decisively to get results that made a difference. The TTW approach Kilts had used for years at Kraft was something he was eager to expose and embed throughout the Gillette organization.

Kilts wanted a top-notch cadre of strategic planners who would formalize the company's new strategies and plans. But even more important, he needed an entire organization—from entry-level managers to the senior executive team—who could think strategically and provide the content that would be shaped into the strategic plans. A global company of Gillette's reach and scope couldn't function if strategic thinking were the province of an elite few who were largely separated from the day-to-day operations of the business. Gillette needed strategic thinkers at every level, in all functions, in all operations, and in all countries. And Gillette, in order to turn itself around completely, needed to eliminate as many of the geographic, cultural, behavioral, attitudinal roadblocks and barriers as possible to create a unified and shared strategic thinking.

This meant that Gillette needed a uniform process for analyzing, dissecting, and prioritizing issues, trends, and marketplace dynamics; for formulating conclusions and then generating goals, strategies, and plans of action. The process must use one clear, common language—with terms that had accepted universal meanings. The lexicon had to be simple to grasp, clear in its meaning, and capable of application worldwide. And the process had to be grounded in core principles to anchor the understanding of what was to be done, yet also provide tools and frameworks to facilitate the results Kilts was after.

Kilts did not want strategic thinking to mean protracted thinking. His mantra was to create a company that was faster, better, and more complete than competitors in delivering consumer value and customer leadership. The TTW process that Kilts introduced grew and evolved at Gillette as it expanded throughout the organization. In a period of two years, TTW reached more than 3,500 managers in more than 70 countries at every management level of the company.

And the results were as impressive as the numbers. Gillette went from the bottom of its peer group to the top. By every measure, it demonstrated how powerful strategic thinking could be. Sales had a compound annual growth rate of 9 percent; earnings were up 14 percent annually; and growth in the stock price added $18 billion to shareholders value. In fact, the company reached a level of performance and excellence that attracted a premium offer from Procter & Gamble (P&G) of more than $57 billion to acquire Gillette.

Anchoring Starts at the Top

Change gets institutionalized when leaders champion it and work the change into ongoing training and development programs. We've already seen how decisively Michelle Stacy worked at Oral-B and Keurig utilizing TTW at both companies. In fact, when Michelle became president of Keurig, one of her first decisions was to instill the Think to Win process into every department of the company, which at the time was more like two companies.

Keurig, which made the individual coffee brewing cups, was founded by a group of entrepreneurs. It was acquired by Green Mountain Coffee Roasters, which also was a small entrepreneurial company. Two years later it was still trying to mesh Keurig with Green Mountain to form a new whole.

"We had two small companies that had come together," says Michelle. "But there was no merging of systems, because neither of them had many systems in place. They were run by extremely bright, entrepreneurial people who were used to putting things together on the kitchen table. If you think about it, entrepreneurs are visionaries. They don't want a lot of structure, and in fact, they spend most of their lives actually avoiding structure. That's why they became successful entrepreneurs."

These entrepreneurs were eager to learn more. So the entire management team went through the Think to Win process, starting at the top of the organization. "It did several things for us," Michelle says. "First, it started to create a discipline about how we would make decisions. Second, it brought a phenomenal training program to the table, which gave these entrepreneurs a really incredible strategic tool. TTW brought groups of 30 people together for two days. It gave everyone the opportunity to not only learn a common language, but also to create team relationships. It got people working together who had never even met before. It was very powerful."

After going through the workshop, even the skeptics became enthusiasts. They discovered that the process didn't stifle creativity; it *channeled* it. The top leadership at Keurig Green Mountain not only went through the training themselves, but they also became faculty, coaches, and mentors to others in the company who attended the workshops after they "graduated."

The shared TTW experience created a common language and approach to how problems were analyzed that helped to integrate Keurig and Green Mountain.

IMPORTANCE OF TRAINING

The word "training" has lost favor in some HR circles. It has been replaced by words such as learning development and talent development. Emphasis is on "development" with experts in the field focusing on skill-building in a fast-paced social media world. While people learn differently, the best way to acquire TTW skills is a classroom training experience followed by quick application back on the job. Training, for example, is how people learn the TTW skill—people have to be trained. The classroom is a safe environment to acquire the skill. The formula is teach, practice, and teach. In a recent session, participants created umbrella statements and brought them to the session. As they went through the TTW training, they learned how to address the issue. They revisited their umbrella statement throughout the training session; and by the time the workshop was over, participants had revised their statement—with coaching from other participants in the class. And they had a renewed sense of confidence on how to tackle the problem using the TTW approach. During the last day of the session, they coached each other and discussed how to take their work back to their jobs.

Meetings—From Wasteful to Productive

Meetings may not be an obvious way to anchor change, especially since so many are unproductive. According to a report by the consulting firm Bain & Company, as much as 15 percent of an organization's time is spent in meetings, a percentage that has increased every year since 2008. Another study showed that more than 50 percent of the time spent in meetings is unproductive. One study estimated that employees can spend up to four hours each week just preparing for status update meetings.

Yet meetings can be a very productive way to solve problems and align resources. The key is to *make* meetings productive. When the executive director of a national nonprofit, adopted the productive meeting approach, she reduced the number of meetings and the participants also found themselves looking forward to attending them. Think to Win has an approach that is outlined below.

TTW Meeting Template

In planning any meeting, we need to ask two key questions:

- ▶ What is the purpose of this meeting?
- ▶ Who needs to attend the meeting?

We need to be guided by five principles:

1. Challenge the assumptions underlying what we are doing.
2. Scope the issues.
3. Focus on the vital few.
4. Acquire a sense of how facts inform outcomes.
5. Provide a linkage that will connect the dots of our plan.

Meeting Guidelines

The following guidelines should be observed:

- ▶ Respect all points of view—remember that everyone has a voice.
- ▶ Come to the meeting prepared—prework is required.
- ▶ Have an agenda with a clear meeting purpose.
- ▶ Honor the presenters—don't allow "sidebar" digressions from the purpose at hand.
- ▶ Stay focused: give technology a rest!
- ▶ Recap decisions and actions.
- ▶ Be on time, and finish on time.

Meeting Process

As the meeting proceeds, we need to ask the following questions and formulate appropriate answers:

1. What do we know?
2. What issues need to be addressed?
3. What decisions need to be made?
4. Follow-ups: Who owns what and by when?

We need to communicate succinctly. Our meeting plan needs to be summarized in key messages focusing in three areas:

- ► What is the basic situation?
- ► What action needs to be undertaken?
- ► What kind of impact will result from this action?

Solving the Accountability Problem

Why is accountability such a universal problem? The main difficulties are that performance management systems don't link what the company is trying to accomplish and what is expected of the individual either because the system is no good or the managers do a bad job of communicating.

It is critical to establish accountability, and there are easy-to-understand tools that directly tie individual objectives to strategies. When one large multinational company anchored the performance process to its growth plan, engagement scores skyrocketed. Following are the important elements identified by an internal Gallup survey for managers establishing clear expectations:

- ► Use the performance management process as a tool for accountability (annual objectives and quarterly priorities) and development (individual development plans).
- ► Delegate responsibility and hold people accountable.
- ► Lead by example.
- ► Use periodic staff meetings to review and refine expectations.

To fully align performance and TTW in the organization, regular feedback to individuals is part of the process. In a recent study of more than 47,000 employed respondents in 116 countries, from Canada to Qatar, the Gallup organization (Steve Crabtree,"What Your Employees Need to Know," *Gallup Business Journal*, April 13, 2011) found performance feedback sorely lacking, which negatively impacts associate engagement and organizational performance.

HAVING THE RIGHT PERFORMANCE MANAGEMENT TOOL

Having the right tool is important. Often the balanced scorecard is used to capture objectives. It directly links the key strategic issues and the organization/department's goals to an individual's personal performance objectives. The balanced scorecard looks at four areas of linked goals that flow from the organization's strategic plan: people, process, consumer/customer and financial. Each quadrant is important and interdependent for achieving the goals established within the other three. See Table 9.1.

TABLE 9.1.　THE BALANCED SCORECARD

Q2 **Process (organizational)results** Accountability examples: ▶ Functional excellence ▶ Process improvement	Q3 **Customer/consumer results** Accountability examples: ▶ Consumer ▶ Customer service
Q1 **People results** Accountability examples: ▶ Acquiring and developing talent ▶ Employee engagement	Q4 **Financial results** Accountability examples: ▶ Efficiency targets ▶ Revenue

Once the balanced scorecard is created, personal performance objectives can be established to align performance up, down, and across an organization that is looking to sustain TTW. Table 9.2 is an example taken from the multinational organization that has embedded TTW into its high-performance culture.

TABLE 9.2.   EXAMPLE OF BALANCED SCORECARD

Area of Accountability	Performance Objectives	Relative Priority	Standard of Performance
1.0 Financial Performance	Maximize the financial health of the overall business by keeping key financial ratios in line with best in class	**30%**	
	1.1 Reduce the net factory variances in all plants		Variances must be kept in line with product cost targets

Source: From D. Ulrich, J. Zenger, and N. Smallwood, *Results-Based Leadership: How Leaders Build Business and Improve the Bottom Line*; Cambridge, MA: Harvard Business School Press, 1999.

Recognition Matters

Recognition matters. Consider Julie's story. Julie, the head of talent development for a pharmaceutical company, was planning an annual retreat for her function. She wanted to recognize her recruiting team members because they were deeply involved in much of the change that had taken place over the last year. The organization was "rightsizing"—continuously shifting and restructuring—adding headcount to one function while eliminating positions in another.

In the midst of the change, the company also bought a pet-care pharmaceutical company, and Julie and her team had to get the new organization up and running. They had less than 60 days to fill more than 25 leadership roles. Using the TTW process, the recruiting team identified the issues and landed on the right choices.

At the retreat, Julie called on the members of her recruiting team and asked them to list the results they delivered. Once they detailed the list, Julie asked a follow-up question: Why was their effort so important to the long-term health of the organization? The ensuing discussion, which highlighted more than a dozen direct and indirect benefits, was so illuminating that Julie shared a reprise with the leaders of the sales group. And they were so impressed that they passed it on to the president of the division.

The result: The division president rewarded the group with a special dinner in which he honored their accomplishments and how they were done. Later that month the recruiting team showcased its use of TTW to the president's direct reports. When people are recognized for the accomplishments resulting from TTW, the approach spreads and becomes part of the company culture.

Rewards can also be used to acknowledge and reinforce change. Rewards can take many forms and are an important lever. Often part of an overall compensation system, rewards can be in the form of salary increases, bonuses, and other types of financial incentives. They can also take other forms including time off to spend with family, gift certificates, and many others things. The key to their effectiveness is tying them to do what's important to the individuals.

HR Practices to Sustain Winning

Management systems that enable sustainable behavior change will work, according to Ulrich and Smallwood, because they "signal, reinforce, and encourage it." (*Leadership Sustainability,* New York: McGraw-Hill, 2013) In any organization or any team, winning cannot occur if leaders are torn between what the organization wants and what they must ultimately do. On the organizational scale, polices that anchor change are found in HR practices. Ulrich and Smallwood summarize these as being present in four flows. (See Table 9.3.)

TABLE 9.3. THE FOUR FLOWS

Area of Flow	How It Sustains Change
Flow of people What happens to the organization's key asset—its people—including how people move in, through, up, and out of the organization	Proper attention to people flow ensures the availability of the talent the organization needs to accomplish its strategy.
Flow of performance management What links people to work—the standards and measures, financial and nonfinancial rewards, and feedback that reflect stakeholder interests	Proper attention to this flow promotes accountability for performance by defining, noting, and rewarding it; and penalizing its absence.

Area of Flow	How It Sustains Change
Flow of information What keeps people aware of the organization and their collective knowledge resources	Proper attention to information flow ensures that people know what is happening and why, and they can apply themselves to what needs doing to create value.
Flow of work Who does work, how work is done, and where work is done combine individual efforts into organizational outputs	Proper attention to workflow provides the governance processes, accountability, and physical setting that ensure high-quality results.

HR Practices Help Sustain Winning

When Dave West was recruited from Hershey's to run Del Monte Foods, he had a track record of success. During his tenure at Hershey's, he had cut costs, consolidated operations, accelerated product innovation, and put Hershey's on a path for success. Dave, a longtime user of TTW, knew that even more change would be needed at Del Monte.

Founded more than a century ago, Del Monte has been one of the largest producers, distributors, and marketers of foods, generating billions in annual sales. For generations, Del Monte was known for its popular lines of canned fruits and vegetables as well as its Contadina Italian-style sauces. Over time, Del Monte's reputation for high-quality products began to morph into a perception that while Del Monte continued to be high quality it also had become old-fashioned, bordering on stodgy. It was one of many factors that made a turnaround and rebirth essential.

Dave and his team recognized that Del Monte needed to increase its investment to build its brands and also reshape its image. As Del Monte's reinvention began, the company was reorganized around four major sectors: operations, growth, finance, and human resources. The vision was to become a best-in-class consumer packaged goods company, with go-to-market and supply chain excellence, underpinned by a high-performance culture and an engaged workforce.

One of the key players that Dave wanted to work with him was an HR executive who could hit the ground running—someone who understood how to think, plan, and act. Importantly, Dave also wanted someone who could speak the TTW language and take on two key challenges: (1) create an HR function that served as a partner to the business in tackling its issues, and (2) create the systems and practices that would help it to win. Dave wanted practices that would not only change the company, but that would also help guide its long-term success.

Dave found the person he was looking for in Asad Husain, a seasoned executive who had used the TTW process while a senior HR executive at the Gillette Company and then at Procter & Gamble. As a member of the HR operating committee at Gillette, he was instrumental in the successful transformation of the Gillette organization during its turnaround. He was also well respected for his role in the integration of Gillette when it was acquired by P&G. Following P&G, Asad had served as the global head of HR at Dun & Bradstreet.

HR plays a critical role in anchoring change in any organization, and Asad Husain faced many issues when he joined Del Monte. There was no comprehensive talent management system to attract, select, develop, plan, and manage a high-performance workforce. Employee turnover was high, and employee engagement was low. Critical managerial vacancies had gone unfilled for months. Plus, the focus of HR had remained largely administrative. Internal surveys showed that HR was overinvested in administrative activities and underinvested in attracting and retaining quality talent. In other words, it was doing a good job on relatively unimportant matters and not reaching expectations on the things that mattered most to the business.

It became clear to Asad that for Del Monte to win, the new human resources capability would have to operate more strategically than it had in the past. It would have to refocus on attracting new talent and building team member engagement at all levels of the company. This meant that he must accomplish two tasks. To achieve the enterprisewide business goal, the HR team had to rise to a different level. To enable the change throughout Del Monte, HR had to focus on all the people systems. To support the Del Monte businesses, changes were required in management systems—talent acquisition, rewards systems, performance systems, and also changes in how HR saw itself, a change in its understanding of the role it played. It had to move swiftly and vigorously from just supporting the current structure to becoming a leader of change throughout the company.

To begin the transformation process, Asad engaged his HR team with the TTW approach, with an overall goal to develop a high-performance HR organization that could help transform Del Monte. He brought his key managers together to conduct a fact-based situation assessment of internal strengths and weaknesses, and external opportunities and threats. They identified key issues and strategies to set up the HR function and deliver business plans. Using this process, Asad got a true picture of what was needed. He knew that if the HR organization didn't think and act differently, it would not be able to meet the changing needs of the business.

He communicated his strategic priorities to Dave West and began to implement the changes. The Del Monte organization tackled each of the following areas of flow by modifying HR practices identified in its strategic plan to accelerate turnaround and sustain winning in the marketplace:

- ▶ **Flow of information.** Used specific communication and training to better provide line of sight and clarity to company's strategic direction and alignment on organizational priorities. Got everyone on same page.
- ▶ **Flow of work.** Focused on why design changes would help strengthen interdependencies and ensure performance linkage. Linked performance measurement to strategic goals across the board by organizing around process and workflow.
- ▶ **Flow of people.** Shifted from disparate process and systems to the Del Monte way—an enterprise approach for talent processes (that is, how to: hire, promote, develop, retain, assess, and so on) with defined linkages (inputs/outputs). Positioned competencies as the foundation for talent management processes (leadership and functional)— change from silos to create an environment where talent is considered to be an enterprise resource and leaders are transparent, collaborative, and act cross-functionally. Established a more formal approach to employee development

by ensuring that all employees have an individual development plan. Some plans will call for accelerated development.

► **Flow of performance management.** Simplified the high-performance culture performance management process for improved goal alignment, accountability, and line of sight to the strategy of the company. Provided additional manager education on effective performance management and coaching.

The result was the creation of a capability that influenced the business and played a significant part in the transformation of the company. And importantly, it set the company up for changes that were to come. Within a year, the company acquired and successfully integrated the Natural Balance business, and the organization was prepared for its bigger role.

Then, in 2014, Del Monte Foods sold its food businesses—and its name—to an unaffiliated company—Del Monte Pacific Ltd. On the day after the sale, the legacy Del Monte operation renamed itself Big Heart Pet Brands and became the largest stand-alone pet food and pet snacks company in North America. With solid HR practices anchored in place, the organization was ready to face the future.

EMMA'S VICTORY: LANDING THE JOB AND GETTING ACCEPTED

After carefully reviewing the spreadsheet that she updates on a three- to five-day basis, Emma begins to apply for jobs. During the first four weeks, she faces a series of ups and downs. Although some of her applications have been accepted and she has several phone and in-person interviews, she doesn't get beyond the initial interviews. It's a turbulent month because of the travel that she does for different interviews in Boston, New York City, and Connecticut.

Emma reaches out to some friends who work in staffing agencies and for recruiting firms. Based on their advice, she changes her approach, seeks a contract position, and secures a temporary spot with a world-class organization.

Emma uses this position to work on her shyness and develop public speaking skills that enable her to develop a "professional voice" with her colleagues. She demonstrates her value by accepting challenges and working long hours. As her value is recognized, she is offered a full-time position, and the organization supports her education goals. So within six months, she is attending admission sessions for graduate schools and sets a date to take the GMAT entrance exam.

Since Emma will be attending school and also working full time, she needs to manage her time wisely. She also needs a strategy to cover the educational costs—how to pay for tuition, books, and other expenses on a limited salary. Emma seeks help from the financial planner made available by her employer and develops a realistic plan. By making the right choices (think: balanced scorecard), she overcomes another hurdle. Her use of the TTW process continues.

Chapter Summary

- ▶ TTW doesn't end with execution. Long-term success calls for the systematic change, embedding it in the culture to sustain and anchor winning results.
- ▶ Skilled use of symbols and signals can help to anchor changes. Often the visual reminders of a symbol can reinforce concepts even more powerfully than words.
- ▶ Change gets institutionalized when leaders champion it and work the change into ongoing training and development programs.
- ▶ Meetings may not be an obvious way to anchor change, especially since so many are unproductive. Yet meetings can be a very productive way to solve problems and align resources. The key is to limit them and make them productive.
- ▶ Establishing accountability is critical, and there are simple, easy-to-understand tools that directly link individual objectives to strategies.
- ▶ Recognition matters. Once people know they are recognized for using TTW, it spreads quickly and becomes part of the company culture.

Chapter 9 Exercises

Mastering Think to Win

We need to focus on change.

Anchoring Change

Anchoring changes into the organization means pushing or pulling levers that drive behavior. TTW provides several powerful tools, each of which helps you think about how to sustain changes in your organization.

Ask the following:

▶ How am I recognizing and rewarding others?
▶ Do we have the policies and procedures in place to help us drive the appropriate behavior?
▶ How are we investing in building TTW capabilities?
▶ What can I learn from the world of sports teams that have been successful over the long run? What mechanism have they put in place to anchor change?

Change is best anchored by the levers that we are able to push in an organization. We have identified what we call soft levers (those that are easier to put in place) and hard levers (those that take much more effort to change). All are important and must be considered as a way to win!

LEVERS THAT ANCHOR CHANGE

"Easier" to Push

▶ Symbols and signals
▶ Training and development
▶ Recognition
▶ Champions and sponsors
▶ Policies, procedures
▶ Communication

"Harder" to Push

► Organizational structure
► Technology and resources
► Physical work environment
► Rewards (compensation)
► Measures and feedback systems
► Values, behaviors, and norms

Exercise: Steps to Anchoring Change
(Can be done at individual or group level)

Choose a lever that needs to be pushed. Identify at least three potential actions that could help improve the way people behave in the organization. Consider the following criteria and assess and rank order your initiatives against the criteria.

► Impact
► Ease of implementation
► Time
► Cost

Choose which actions you are recommending and why:

► Discuss
► Review for clarity
► Align on action

The deliverable are actions that can be put in place to help anchor changes.

Organizational Assessment

Use the following table as a checklist for identifying TTW principles and practices. This will help you to better understand where you and your team need to focus your energies. To get an idea where you believe your organization stands, read through each statement and jot down a rating:

Concept/Process	Scale: 1 = Low, 5 = High
Time spent in meetings is valued as a way to think and solve problems	
We use rituals and symbols to drive and anchor changes into the organization	
Rewards and recognition systems are tied to behavior and results that the organization needs to be successful	
Our leaders create a tradition of excellence by installing essential processes, routines, and mechanisms to sustain success	
Our people development strategy (workshops, coaching, and on-the-job development) focuses on the knowledge and skills that will help people analyze issues, create solutions, and execute them efficiently and effectively	

Review individual items. Look for items where you scored lower (3 and below) and think about the following questions:

- ▶ What do I believe is driving the score?
- ▶ What do I need to stop, start, or continue doing?
- ▶ What do I hope the result to be?

Turning Over the Hourglass

As the poet and dramatist T. S. Eliot said: "What we call the beginning is often the end. And to make an end is to make a beginning. The end is where we start from." (*Four Quartets*, T. S. Eliot, New York: Harcourt, 1943) That thought certainly captures a basic truth about TTW. The process has an end that actually represents a beginning. For once we've completed the TTW process, we either start on a new issue or challenge or make plans in the future to reassess a previous issue.

And for the future, TTW's relevance will be large. On a trip to the Harvard Innovation Center where some of the top young minds in the world explore innovative, cutting-edge approaches to entrepreneurial start-ups, an executive in residence, a long-time user of TTW, noted how relevant and important the TTW process would be in the center.

"Could you imagine a young entrepreneur working through an idea without asking questions such as, What do we know? What is most important? What conclusions can we make? What might the implications be? All thinking—whether far out and daring or near in and conservative—has to be framed within a process that provides discipline and direction—a process that works.

Her observations suggest another value that TTW will provide in the years ahead—a common language and uniform approach that will serve to bridge generational differences. In their book *The 2020 Workplace,* Jeanne Meister and Karie Willyerd (New York: Harper Business, 2010) describe a workplace with five very culturally and attitudinally different generations of people working side by side: Traditionalists (born before 1946); Baby Boomers (born between 1946 and 1964); Generation X (born between 1965 and 1976); Millennials (born between 1977 and 1997); and Generation 2020 (born after 1997). TTW serves to orient everyone's thinking to a fact-based, structured process with a common language regardless of generation.

As companies in the future look for ways to enhance their performance, TTW offers great value. Within a corporate strategic planning process, the value of TTW may even be greater than the typical strategic plan itself. In their article "Tired of Strategic Planning" (*McKinsey Quarterly*, June 2002), Eric D. Beinhocker and Sara Kaplan indicate that their research shows that many companies get little value from their annual strategic planning process. One mismatch is the effort required and results achieved from the annual strategy review. The review "frequently amounts to little more than a stage on which business unit leaders present warmed over updates of last year's presentations, take a few risks in broaching new ideas, and strive above all to avoid embarrassment." What the process should be doing is preparing executives to face uncertainties and think creatively about the company's vision and direction. Learning how to think strategically is most important, which is what TTW is all about. TTW provides a flexible yet structured approach that leads to better strategic options.

In his book *Simply Effective,* Ron Ashkenas (Cambridge, MA: Harvard Business Review Press, 2009) says there is no perfect strategy or strategic plan. But TTW provides a greater sense of confidence in the choices to be made.

On a personal level, our book shows Emma's use of TTW for career planning. We've also compiled a list of the top 20 personal TTW applications based on our observations and experiences:

1. Buying a house
2. Landscaping your new home
3. Remodeling your house
4. Planning a wedding
5. Starting a family
6. Starting a career/job search
7. Starting a business/organization/club
8. Moving to a different city, state, or even country
9. Coaching a sports team
10. Identifying the right college for a child
11. Buying the right car
12. Losing weight/changing your looks
13. Running in a marathon
14. Building a sports organization
15. Improving your golf game
16. Writing a book
17. Investing for the future
18. Planning a dream vacation
19. Planning for retirement
20. Selling a house

Finally, as we have shown with several illustrations in this book, the TTW process works as well with nonprofits as it does with businesses. Our training sessions for volunteer workers with nonprofits always have an impact on the individuals as well as the organization. The following is a transformational story of how one church used the TTW process to bring a rebirth to its parish.

Father Joe, a farsighted priest who leads a New England parish, wanted to explore ways to ensure its future vibrancy. At the suggestion of one of his parishioners, he decided to use TTW, and he started by reaching out to a variety of people in his congregation who had the skills or interests that would add value to the planning process. This planning group began with an internal and external analysis, looking at strengths, weaknesses, opportunities, and threats. "We shared the history of the parish, and conducted a thorough analysis of our organization and of the changing world around us," says Father Joe. "We looked at our town and nation, our archdiocese and the larger church. We identified areas of growth and concern. This process involved a good deal of research, discussion, questioning, and clarifying, and took a little over a year."

With its situation assessment completed, the group identified its key issues. Starting from a list of 15, it landed on 7, which included what demographic groups—elders and youngsters; active members, and the disenfranchised—how to make members more active; how to identify families in crisis; how to establish a new model of the church that relied on an increased role for the laity (a less pastor-centric model), and how to identify ways to increase the financial support necessary for future growth.

"There was a lot of interest, and even a little concern as we talked about the pastoral care issue, what some called a new model of the church," says Father Joe. "It may sound kind of hackneyed, but this is not the church that most of us grew up in. This is a whole different moment. Those in leadership were aware, but the issue was how to make the larger parish community aware. How do we move people beyond, "Oh, I *go* to church," to, "I *am* the church"?

The empowerment of the laity was a big aha moment for there is a shortage of ordained priests throughout the country and in this parish in particular. Father Joe once had several priests on staff; now he had only one, even though his congregation was growing. The planning group realized that a transition was necessary from a top-down, pastor-centered church to a congregation collaborative model where leadership was shared and managed by volunteers.

The planning group set up seven teams, one for each priority. Each team drafted a team charter that identified its scope and objectives, and in particular what members would focus on in the immediate future and what they would accomplish over the next three years.

The church soon began taking action in response to the priorities. The parish instituted a monthly ROC (rely on Christ) mass to solidify and enhance its connection with teens and young adults. It began holding regular workshops on depression and anxiety, and it set up a career transition ministry to help the unemployed find new jobs. The parish also established a new system to take in donations. The financial stability team had sought to blunt the impact of weekly fluctuations in revenue. If the New England weather was very bad—or very good—or if there had been an outbreak of colds or flu, fewer people attended mass on Sunday. "They encouraged parishioners to give on a monthly basis, rather than contributing at Sunday mass," says Father Joe. "At their suggestion, we also initiated online giving."

The innovations and changes continue. "If human change is difficult, imagine change within a 2,000-year institution that has prided itself on 'we've always done it this way,'" says Father Joe. "The strategic thinking process taps into the energy of the community and the many gifts of our members to help enable significant change."

Turning over the hourglass certainly makes a difference.

Organizational Alignment Survey

This survey (copyright © by GlobalEd, LLC) is designed to assess effectiveness for thinking about business issues and aligning and executing strategies to drive growth. It offers an opportunity for you to get a high-level assessment of your organization's strategic thinking capability.

Respond to each of the following statements by checking the number that most accurately reflects your view of that statement. If you believe the statement absolutely reflects your organization or unit, select column 5. If you believe the statement does not reflect your organization or unit at all, select column 1.

Challenging Assumptions

Having an open mind and being willing to challenge accepted beliefs and raise new concerns.

1. We are open to new ways that explore our previously held beliefs.

Strongly disagree	O 1	O 2	O 3	O 4	O 5	Strongly agree

2. We have a willingness to challenge existing assumptions.

Strongly disagree	O 1	O 2	O 3	O 4	O 5	Strongly agree

3. Our organization encourages us to express any and all of our views, even if we disagree with top management.

Strongly disagree	O 1	O 2	O 3	O 4	O 5	Strongly agree

4. We challenge existing assumptions as a mechanism for identifying new business opportunities.

Strongly disagree	O 1	O 2	O 3	O 4	O 5	Strongly agree

Vital Few

Focus on the vital few issues rather than tackling everything. Analyzing and concluding effectively enhances clarity, directs focus, and promotes balance.

5. We thoroughly understand the issues we need to address before we make decisions on goals/strategies and plans.

Strongly disagree	O 1	O 2	O 3	O 4	O 5	Strongly agree

6. We identify critical issues and prioritize them effectively.

Strongly disagree	O 1	O 2	O 3	O 4	O 5	Strongly agree

7. We know how to streamline from many to the few key issues.

Strongly disagree	O 1	O 2	O 3	O 4	O 5	Strongly agree

8. We prioritize our efforts around the appropriate business issues that will create clear direction.

Strongly disagree	O 1	O 2	O 3	O 4	O 5	Strongly agree

Facts Versus Opinions

Use facts to make decisions and reach meaningful, valid conclusions; opinions and conjecture do not provide accurate support.

9. In our analysis of information, we are effective in discriminating between fact and opinion.

Strongly disagree	O 1	O 2	O 3	O 4	O 5	Strongly agree

10. Recommendations are based on facts.

Strongly disagree	O 1	O 2	O 3	O 4	O 5	Strongly agree

11. We avoid conjecture by employing facts when making decisions.

Strongly disagree	O 1	O 2	O 3	O 4	O 5	Strongly agree

Scope

Determine the appropriate "scope of analysis" to address the right issues within your control.

12. We are able to clearly and consistently define our most significant business issues in one to two sentences.

Strongly Disagree	O 1	O 2	O 3	O 4	O 5	Strongly Agree

13. We know where to direct our efforts when we begin talking about important issues.

Strongly Disagree	O 1	O 2	O 3	O 4	O 5	Strongly Agree

14. Our managers and supervisors are able to see the "big picture," even in the midst of day-to-day tasks and problems.

Strongly Disagree	O 1	O 2	O 3	O 4	O 5	Strongly Agree

15. We are aware of the scale (organization, function, team) of the issues we are addressing.

Strongly Disagree	O 1	O 2	O 3	O 4	O 5	Strongly Agree

16. We consistently address business issues that are within our control.

Strongly Disagree	O 1	O 2	O 3	O 4	O 5	Strongly Agree

Linkage

Connecting ideas both upstream and downstream allows for systematic thinking; what's up front informs what is to follow.

17. We leverage our internal strengths when making decisions about our business strategies.

Strongly Disagree	O 1	O 2	O 3	O 4	O 5	Strongly Agree

18. Project plans link to strategies and have clear accountabilities.

Strongly Disagree	O 1	O 2	O 3	O 4	O 5	Strongly Agree

19. Our company's core strategies are based on a careful review of our strengths, weaknesses, opportunities, and challenges.

Strongly Disagree	O 1	O 2	O 3	O 4	O 5	Strongly Agree

20. Our organization is aligned to the strategies that we are pursuing.

Strongly Disagree	O 1	O 2	O 3	O 4	O 5	Strongly Agree

21. Our organization consistently delivers on our commitments to each other, our organization, and all of our stakeholders.

Strongly Disagree	O 1	O 2	O 3	O 4	O 5	Strongly Agree

Process

A structured approach that employs a common language for identifying business issues.

22. We use one business language with terms that are clear and simple to grasp.

Strongly Disagree	O 1	O 2	O 3	O 4	O 5	Strongly Agree

23. We use a common approach throughout the organization to drive change.

Strongly Disagree	O 1	O 2	O 3	O 4	O 5	Strongly Agree

24. Our organization has a consistent process for agreeing on deliverables and accountability.

Strongly Disagree	O 1	O 2	O 3	O 4	O 5	Strongly Agree

25. We consistently utilize a process for analyzing and prioritizing issues throughout all levels of the organization.

Strongly Disagree	O 1	O 2	O 3	O 4	O 5	Strongly Agree

Assessment

Routinely assessing internal and external issues that lead to conclusions and implications for action.

26. We use a set of tools for data collection and organization.

Strongly Disagree	O 1	O 2	O 3	O 4	O 5	Strongly Agree

27. We are able to articulate our competitive advantage(s) in the marketplace.

Strongly Disagree	O 1	O 2	O 3	O 4	O 5	Strongly Agree

28. Our company can clearly describe what makes us better than or different from our competitors.

Strongly Disagree	O 1	O 2	O 3	O 4	O 5	Strongly Agree

29. Our company has a process in place to assess our company's strengths and weaknesses that is conducted on a regular basis.

Strongly Disagree	O 1	O 2	O 3	O 4	O 5	Strongly Agree

30. Our organization reviews our performance against deliverables and accountabilities on a regular basis.

Strongly Disagree	O 1	O 2	O 3	O 4	O 5	Strongly Agree

Planning

Creating strategies, measures, and developing initiatives that will successfully address overarching business issues.

31. Our company has established measurable goals and targets, as well as timelines for us to realistically expect results.

Strongly Disagree	O 1	O 2	O 3	O 4	O 5	Strongly Agree

32. Our company has a process to ensure that every team has well-developed goals, objectives, and timelines that document their purpose, actions, and results.

Strongly Disagree	O 1	O 2	O 3	O 4	O 5	Strongly Agree

33. Our strategies are clear choices that are based on thorough analyses and insights.

Strongly Disagree	O 1	O 2	O 3	O 4	O 5	Strongly Agree

34. We are able to clearly articulate the strategic choices we need to make to support our goals.

Strongly Disagree	O 1	O 2	O 3	O 4	O 5	Strongly Agree

35. Our organization's current strategies give us a clear advantage over the competition.

Strongly Disagree	O 1	O 2	O 3	O 4	O 5	Strongly Agree

Think to Win Situation Assessment Diagnostic: Situation Assessment Tool for Consumer/ Customer Marketing

Overview

This tool provides a framework for assessing how well you and your organization are marketing your business and brand(s) in the categories in which they compete. The information collected also considers both internal and external factors that will have a significant impact in determining what roles alternative growth programs will play in the future of how your brand(s) are marketed to consumers/customers (e.g., the use of digital/social media, the role of internal new product development, and external development actions such as licensing). It is not intended to be all-inclusive. You may need to customize it to your industry, marketplace, competitive, and internal and external situation. The tool includes a series of questions in six areas of focus:

1. Business objectives/current state of the business
2. Category dynamics
3. Competitive frame
4. Consumer insights
5. Value proposition and delivery
6. Functional advantages

This information will also help identify internal strengths and weaknesses plus external opportunities and threats to determine the key issues you must address for your business and brand(s).

TABLE B.1.   BUSINESS OBJECTIVES/CURRENT STATE OF THE BUSINESS

Question	Answer Choices		
1. How would you describe your company's role in the industry/category? *(Check all that apply)*	❏ Share leader ❏ Profitable niche player ❏ Innovator ❏ Fast follower ❏ Premium/high-end player	❏ Overall value player ❏ Lowest-cost producer ❏ Highest-quality producer ❏ Customer service leader ❏ Other	
2. How has your company performed *in sales growth* **over the last three years?**	❏ Met internal targets ❏ Surpassed internal targets ❏ Fell short of internal targets		Average annual *company* sales growth rate: ____%

Question	Answer Choices		
3. Compared to the rest of the industry/ category, how has your company performed in sales growth?	❑ Lead in growth ❑ Comparable performance ❑ Weaker performance		Average annual *industry* sales growth rate: ____%
4. What have been the principal drivers of your *sales* performance? *(Check all that apply)*	❑ Overall industry performance ❑ New products ❑ New lines of business ❑ Gaining new customers ❑ Improved consumer benefit delivery ❑ Improved customer service ❑ Increased competition	❑ Distribution gains ❑ New investments, please specify _____ _____ _____ ❑ Improved marketing ❑ Strategic alliances and partnerships ❑ Shifts in consumer demand, please specify _____ _____ _____	❑ Executional challenges, please specify _____ _____ ❑ Organizational challenges, please specify _____ _____ ❑ Other, please specify _____ _____ _____

5. Have there been significant missed growth opportunities for your company?
____Yes____No
If yes, what were they? Why do you think the company failed to anticipate/leverage these opportunities? _____
_____

Question	Answer Choices		
6. How has your company performed in *profitability* over the last three years?	❑ Met internal targets ❑ Surpassed internal targets ❑ Fell short of internal targets		Average annual *company* profit growth rate: ____%
7. Compared to the rest of the industry/ category, how has your company performed in *profitability*?	❑ Lead in growth ❑ Comparable performance ❑ Weaker performance		Average annual *industry* profit growth rate: ____%
8. What have been the principal drivers of your *profit* performance? *(Check all that apply)*	❑ Overall industry performance ❑ Shift in product mix ❑ High-value consumer gains ❑ Increased competition ❑ Increased retailer clout	❑ New investments, please specify _____ _____ ❑ Marketing costs ❑ R&D costs ❑ Manufacturing costs ❑ Selling and administrative costs	❑ Executional efficiencies/ inefficiencies, please specify _____ _____ ❑ Organizational efficiencies/ inefficiencies, please specify _____ _____ ❑ Other, please specify _____ _____ _____

TABLE B.1.   BUSINESS OBJECTIVES/CURRENT STATE OF THE BUSINESS
(CONTINUED)

Question	Answer Choices		
9. What are your sales and profit objectives going forward?		Average annual *projected sales* growth rate: ___%	Average annual *projected profit* growth rate: ___%
10. What is the strategic value to your business of going online? **Rank categories 1 to 7** *1 = most strategic;* *7 = least strategic*	Incremental revenue — Direct sales to current customers — Cross selling/up-selling to current customers — Direct sales to new customers — Affiliate sales Enhanced consumer loyalty — Customer service — Information/content — Community building	Marketing leverage — Direct marketing — On line promotions Market research leverage — Consumer profiling — New product testing	Inventory management leverage — Supply/sourcing leverage — Other, please specify _____ _____ _____
11. What percentage of sales and profits do you expect your online business to contribute on an ongoing basis?		Average projected *sales* contribution of online business: ___%	Average projected *profit* contribution of online business: ___%
12. What can you leverage from your existing business that makes going online a compelling proposition? _____			

TABLE B.2.   CATEGORY DYNAMICS

Question	Answer Choices		
1. What has been the state of category growth over the last three years? *(Check all that apply)*	❑ Flat/no growth ❑ Significant increase in growth ❑ Marginal increase in growth	❑ Significant decline ❑ Marginal decline ❑ Increasing growth momentum	❑ Decreasing growth momentum ❑ Accelerating decline ❑ Decelerating decline
2. How much have the following factors affected category dynamics to date? *Please rate each on a scale of 1 to 5 (5 being the highest)* **5 = Very High Impact** **1 = Very Low Impact**	— Shifts in consumer demand (e.g., attitudes and motivations, behavior, demographics) — Changes in the competitive frame (e.g., new competitors, new substitutes)	— Changes in retail dynamics — Regulatory changes	— Technological advancements — Product technologies — Packaging technologies — Marketing technologies — Other broad-based

Question	Answer Choices

3. For factors rated 5, please indicate what these changes/advancements have been.

_____

_____

_____

---

4. What is the outlook for category growth over the next three years?

(Check all that apply)

❏ Flat/no growth
❏ Significant increase in growth
❏ Marginal increase in growth

❏ Significant decline
❏ Marginal decline
❏ Increasing growth momentum

❏ Decreasing growth momentum
❏ Accelerating decline
❏ Decelerating decline

---

5. What are the emerging areas of growth?

(Check all that apply)

❏ Consumer needs to be met, please specify
_____
_____

❏ Consumer segments to serve, please specify
_____
_____

❏ Product platforms to offer, please specify
_____
_____

❏ Distribution avenues to access, please specify
_____
_____

❏ Geographic expansion please specify
_____
_____

❏ Other, please specify
_____
_____

---

6. How much do you anticipate will the following factors affect *future* category dynamics?

Please rate each on a scale of 1 to 5 (5 being the highest)

5 = Very High Impact
1 = Very Low Impact

— Shifts in consumer demand (e.g., attitudes and motivations, behavior, demographics)
— Changes in the competitive frame (e.g., new competitors, new substitutes)

— Changes in retail dynamics
— Regulatory changes

— Technological advancements
  — Product technologies
  — Packaging technologies
  — Marketing technologies
  — Other broad-based

---

7. For factors rated 5, please indicate what you *expect* these changes/advancements to be.

_____

_____

_____

---

8. How does going online help you exploit/leverage these factors to your advantage?

_____

_____

_____

---

9. How well does your company anticipate emerging demand?

Please rate on a scale of 1 to 5 (5 being the highest)

❏ 1
❏ 2
❏ 3

❏ 4
❏ 5

TABLE B.3. COMPETITIVE FRAME

Question	Answer Choices		
1. Who are your top three key competitors? *Please indicate by rank*	**Competitor** 1._____ 2._____ 3._____	**Performance** ___Gaining share ___Flat ___Losing share ___Gaining share ___Flat ___Losing share ___Gaining share ___Flat ___Losing share	
How would you characterize their performance in the last three years?			
2. What do you know about the strategies of each competitor?	**Competitor** 1._____ 2._____ 3._____	**Current Strategies** 1._____ 2._____ 3._____	**Implied Future Strategies** 1._____ 2._____ 3._____
3. What is the basis of competition in your industry/ category? *Please rate the importance of each on a scale of 1 to 5 (5 being the highest)*	— Product breadth — Product depth — Advertising — Promotions — Innovation	— Branding — Technology — Customer service — Pricing — Quality/performance	— Distribution — Low cost delivery/ manufacturing — Other _____
4. Which competitor, yourself included, performs best in each of these competitive factors?	Product breadth _____ Product depth _____ Advertising _____ Innovation _____	Branding _____ Technology _____ Customer service _____ Pricing _____	Distribution _____ Low cost delivery/ manufacturing _____ Other (specify) _____
5. How uniquely advantaged are you in each of these competitive factors? *Please rate each on a scale of 1 to 5 (5 being the highest)*	— Product breadth — Product depth — Advertising — Promotions — Innovation	— Branding — Technology — Customer service — Pricing — Quality/performance	— Distribution — Low cost delivery/ manufacturing — Other (specify) _____

Question	Answer Choices
6. How does going online help you exploit/leverage these competitive factors to your advantage? _____ _____ _____	

| **7. How does your competitive frame change in the online environment?** | **Potential New Competitors**
 1._____

 2._____

 3._____ | **Implied Strategies**
 1._____

 2._____

 3._____ |

8. How can you differentiate your company against this new competitive set?
_____   _____   _____

TABLE B.4.   CONSUMER INSIGHTS

Question	Answer Choices	
1. How well do you understand consumers in your industry/ category? _Please check one on a scale of 1 to 5_ _1 = We have little understanding_ _5 = We have proprietary insights the competition doesn't have_	❏ 1 ❏ 2 ❏ 3	❏ 4 ❏ 5
2. What is your level of understanding about consumers in your industry/category on each of the following dimensions? _Please rate each on a scale of 1 to 5:_ _1 = We have little understanding_ _5 = We have proprietary insights the competition doesn't have_	___ Attitudes and motivations ___ Benefits sought ___ Purchase criteria ___ Usage of the category (e.g., frequency, products/services used) ___ Brand beachheads/ loyalty	___ Channel behaviors ___ Demographics ___ Lifestyle

(Continues)

TABLE B.4. CONSUMER INSIGHTS *(CONTINUED)*

Question	Answer Choices
3. Who are your target consumers? _____ _____ _____	
4. How many segments do you target? _____ _____ _____	
5. What percentage of the target are heavy users?___ **What percentage of sales/profit do they represent?**___	

6. How does your target feel about technology?
 	
   a. **What percent is online?**____
 	
   b. **What percent shop online?**____
 	
   c. **What else do the majority do online? (e.g., e-mail, find information, etc.)**
 _____
 _____	

7. How loyal do you think your target consumers are to your brand? *Please rate on a scale 1 to 5 (5 being the highest)*	❑ 1 ❑ 4 ❑ 2 ❑ 5 ❑ 3
8. Which of these does your target consumer require/need from your product and your company?	Product offering _____ Service offering _____ Benefits delivered _____ Price _____ Channel access _____ Marketing _____ Other _____

Question	Answer Choices	
9. How well do you do in delivering their requirements? *Please rate each one on a scale of 1 to 5 (5 being the highest)*	— Product offering — Service offering — Benefits delivered — Price	— Channel access — Marketing — Other (specify) _____
10. How *uniquely* do you serve them on each of these requirements? *Please rate each one on a scale of 1 to 5 (5 being the highest)*	— Product offering — Service offering — Benefits delivered — Price	— Channel access — Marketing — Other (specify) _____
11. What are you doing to *uniquely* serve your target consumers in *any* of the following?	Product offering _____ Service offering _____ Benefits delivered _____ Price _____ Channel access _____ Marketing _____ Other _____	

12. Please check those statements below that apply to your target consumer:

- ❏ Accounts for largest volume share in the category/is the heavy user in the category
- ❏ Is the most profitable segment to serve
- ❏ Is most involved/has greatest affinity for the category
- ❏ Has upside volume potential/Is the source of future demand in the category
- ❏ Is driven by benefits versus price
- ❏ Is intensely sought after by other competitors
- ❏ Is driven by benefits we can compete with
- ❏ We have strong advantages to serve the segment
- ❏ Is growing
- ❏ Is a dying breed
- ❏ Is cost-driven

(Continues)

TABLE B.4.   CONSUMER INSIGHTS *(CONTINUED)*

Question	Answer Choices
13. Based on your assessment above, is your current target consumer the ideal/most valuable consumer segment to target in your category? ____Yes If yes, proceed to Question 15. ____No If no, continue with Question 14. _____ _____	
14. What do you need to do to serve and win over this ideal/high-value consumer target in *any* of the following?	Product offering _____ Service offering _____ Benefits delivered _____ Price _____ Channel access _____ Marketing _____ Other _____
15. Is your online target consumer the same or different from your current core franchise? ____If same, proceed to Table B.5, Question 1. ____If different, proceed to Question 16. _____ _____	

Question	Answer Choices
16. How different are your online consumer targets from your core in *any* of the following? ***Please rate each on a scale of from 1 to 5:*** ***1 = quite similar*** ***5 = very different***	____Attitudes and motivations (what drives them to do what they do) ____Benefits sought (what they look for in your product/service) ____Purchase criteria (what drives their brand choice in your category) ____Usage of the category (how often they use products in the category, what types of products/services they use) ____Brand beachheads (what brands they are loyal to right now) ____Channel behavior (what channels they access for the category) ____Demographics (age, gender, income, education, etc.) ____Lifestyle (general interests, way of life)
17. What do you need to deliver differently to this online target in *any* of the following?	Product offering _____ Service offering _____ Benefits delivered _____ Price _____ Channel access _____ Marketing _____ Other (specify) _____ _____

TABLE B.5.   VALUE PROPOSITION AND DELIVERY

Questions	Answer Choices		
1. What is your current value proposition? _____			
Think of the top five benefits you deliver to your consumers and/or the five things you stand for in their minds: a. _____ b. _____ c. _____ d. _____ e. _____			
2. How relevant is your value proposition to your target? *Please rate on a scale of 1 to 5 (5 being the highest)*	❏ 1 ❏ 2 ❏ 3	❏ 4 ❏ 5	Why? _____ _____ _____
3. How unique and differentiated is your value proposition from your competitors'? *Please rate on a scale of 1 to 5 (5 being the highest)*	❏ 1 ❏ 2 ❏ 3	❏ 4 ❏ 5	Why? _____ _____ _____
	❏		
4. How are you currently delivering on each plank of your value proposition (e.g., with what products and services)? *Please rate on a scale of 1 to 5 (5 being the highest or best delivery on value system)*	**Value Proposition Plank** 1._____ 2._____ 3._____ 4._____ 5._____		**Key Initiatives to Deliver** _____ _____ _____ _____ _____

Questions	Answer Choices		
5. How well does your total portfolio of initiatives address your target's benefit requirements? *Please rate on a scale of 1 to 5 (5 being the highest)*	❑ 1 ❑ 2 ❑ 3	❑ 4 ❑ 5	Why? _____ _____ _____
6. How differentiated is your portfolio offering from that of the competitions'? *Please rate on a scale of 1 to 5 (5 being the highest)*	❑ 1 ❑ 2 ❑ 3	❑ 4 ❑ 5	
7. What are drivers of that differentiation? *Check all that apply*	❑ Product/service quality ❑ Product/service breadth ❑ Product/service depth ❑ Benefits delivered, please specify _____ _____		❑ Product/service innovation ❑ Price ❑ Value ❑ Other _____
8. How sustainable is this differentiation? *Please rate on a scale of 1 to 5 (5 being the highest)*	❑ 1 ❑ 2 ❑ 3	❑ 4 ❑ 5	Why? _____ _____ _____

9. Based on the preceding assessment, what are potential gaps in your current offering? For current and future demand alignment? ❑ Product gaps _____ ❑ Service gaps _____ ❑ Benefit/positioning gaps _____ ❑ Performance gaps _____
10. How does going online change your value proposition and/or help you better deliver your value proposition? _____ _____ _____
11. How are your points of differentiation transferable/leveragable online? _____ _____ _____

TABLE B.6.   COMPETENCIES/CORE SKILLS

Question	Answer Choices	
1. What do you perceive as your major strengths and weaknesses?	**Strengths** 1._____ 2._____ 3._____ 4._____ 5._____	**Weaknesses** 1._____ 2._____ 3._____ 4._____ 5._____
2. How would you rate your competencies in the following areas compared to the rest of the industry? *Please rate on a scale of 1 to 5 (5 being industry lead))*	**Functional Advantages** __ R&D __ Sales __ Marketing __ Consumer research __ New business development __ Distribution __ Other (explain) _____ _____	**Business System Advantages** __ Quality of people __ Business processes (e.g., innovation/NPD) __ Culture __ Organizational structure __ Other (explain) _____ _____
3. How well do your competencies support your value proposition to the target consumer? *Please rate on a scale of 1 to 5 (5 being the highest)*	❏ 1 ❏ 4 ❏ 2 ❏ 5 ❏ 3	Why? _____ _____ _____
4. How can you build/leverage these equities and competencies by going online? _____ _____ _____		

Glossary

conclusions: The most important "takeaways" from the situation assessment. A statement that explains the significance of the findings and increases understanding; a short list of five to seven items that must be addressed in the near future.

findings: Conditions found that are based on facts or observations and that are clearly sourced as either fact-based or observation-based. These conditions test the validity of a hypothesis. They often lead to an insight and/or conclusion. They are a descriptive, meaningful answer to a key question. They summarize the central theme of the supporting facts or observations.

frameworks: Tools used to put the facts of the current situation into meaningful compartments. An example is the *seven Cs framework:* company and colleagues (internal); category, customer, consumer, competitors, and community (external). Compartmentalizing facts into a framework adds meaning and relevance to what may appear to be unconnected facts. Frameworks are a bridge to the next part of the situation analysis—the SWOT analysis.

goal: A statement in outcome language of what's to be achieved. It's quantitative in nature and is usually set for three years. A goal answers the question, "What do we want to achieve?"

hypothesis: A tentative conclusion about a problem or opportunity.

implications: The "so what" of the key issues; they are action-oriented responses to each key issue. They describe what the conclusions mean. They can include: What we should do and why. They are not quantified at this stage.

initiatives: Programs, projects, plans ,or activities. They are prioritized annually and are accomplished to bring a strategy to life. Individuals or groups are the sponsors of Initiatives and responsible for their advancement.

key issues: Define the mega problem element—the most controversial problem element; the keystone problem element—a problem element that is "ready." for resolution.

objectives: Specific, measurable statements of what will be done to achieve goals within a time frame. Objectives are achieved through work plans. Work plans delineate who will do what by when, and they include measurements of success or desired outcomes.

SCAs (sustainable competitive advantages):   Superstrengths. They are what truly separate us from the pack. They are our key leverage and margin in the marketplace, and must meet five criteria:

- ▶ Meaningful—significant
- ▶ Add value—confer tangible consumer/customer benefits
- ▶ Hard to imitate—competitive advantage
- ▶ Have the capability of being leveraged—extendable across multiple businesses
- ▶ Sustainable—endure, when nurtured.

strategies: A road map of where to go. They include statements of the major approach to follow to attain goals and resolve issues. Strategies answer the question: How will we go about accomplishing our goals? Strategies describe a general approach or method. They don't describe specific activities or projects. Strategies are choices. There are three types: core strategies, contingency strategies (plan B), and alternative strategies (considered but rejected).

structured analysis: The organized and logical separation, examination, arrangement, and interrelation of the component parts of a problem or area of investigation.

SWOT (strengths, weaknesses, opportunities, and threats): A strategic planning tool, used as part of an environmental scan. More specifically, the process involves identifying meaningful and prioritized factors. The SWOT is a powerful way to summarize an internal and external analysis.

tactics: Describe specific tasks or steps that will advance an initiative.

INDEX

Accountability
  change and, 171, 179
  for execution, 128–129, 134, 137
  of managers, 154
  matrix, 128–129
  meetings and, 171
Actionable insights, 74–75
Actionable vision, 84, 95
Actions. *See also* Execution
  challenges of, 117–119
  in key messages, 140–143, 160
  in management style, 153
  for strategies, 117–119, 121, 132–133
Affordability, 73–74
Affordable Care Act, 89
Aha moments, 102–104
Alignment
  between compensation and vision, 146
  linkage and, 154
  in organizational alignment survey,
    189–195
  plan-on-a-page and, 144, 152
  show of thumbs for, 122–123
  on situation assessment, 150
  on umbrella statements, 43–44, 68, 70
All Clean, 55–57
Alpro, 89
Alternative strategies, 114
Anchoring. *See* Change, anchoring of
Anecdotes, 20
Annual plan, 151–152, 184
Ashkenas, Ron, 184
Assessment. *See also* Organizational
    assessment; Situation Assessment
    Diagnostic
  in organizational alignment survey,
    193–194
  situation, 48, 73, 118, 150, 186, 198–210

Assumptions
  challenging, 16–18, 32–33, 35, 37,
    189–190
  team charter, 120–121, 133
Auriemma, Geno, 163–164
Autonomy, 157
Avon Products, 146
Baby boomers, 184
Baby food, 119–121, 123–128
Balanced goals, 90–92, 95, 97–99
Balanced scorecard, 93–94, 98, 171–172
Barriers, 107, 125
Basketball, 163–164
Batteries, 6–9, 25, 56
Beinhocker, Eric D., 184
Berra, Yogi, 83
BetterFace, 108–112
Big Heart Pet Brands, 178
Big-box stores, 28–30
BlackBerry, 12
Blockbuster, 11, 20
Bologna, 72
Bossidy, Larry, 117–118
Brainstorming, 102–103
Brand
  company, 27–30
  low awareness of, 77
  marketing, 28, 154
  in Total Brand Value, 154
Braun, 87–88
Brazil, 69, 86–87
Brewster, Daryl, 73–74
Bricks-and-mortar model, 11
Business model, 71
Business objectives/current state of the
    business, 198–200

Campbell Soup Company, 145–146

Cash flow, 71
Casual meeting, 159
Category, in seven Cs, 48, 61
Category dynamics, 200–201
Challenge assumptions
  in organizational alignment survey,
    189–190
  principle of, 16–18, 32–33, 35, 37,
    189–190
Challenges
  accepting, 153
  of actions, 117–119
  in goals, 94–95
Change, anchoring of
  accountability and, 171, 179
  Auriemma and, 163–164
  balanced scorecard and, 171–172
  culture and, 149, 179
  Dorrance and, 163–164
  exercises, 179–182
  global anchoring, 166–167
  HR practices and, 174–178
  leaders and, 164–165
  levers for, 180
  organizational assessment of,
    181–182
  productive meetings and, 169–173, 179
  recipe for, 165
  recognition and, 173–174, 179
  steps to, 181
  summarized, 179
  symbols and signals in, 165, 179
  at top, 168–169
  training and, 169
Charan, Ram, 117–118
Chrysler, 140
Church, TTW for, 185–187
Coca-Cola Company, 107
Coffee, 10, 43, 72–73, 85, 88, 105.
    See also Keurig
Cohen, Gary, 42–43, 53
Collaborators, 128–129, 138, 152
Colleagues, in seven Cs, 48, 61
Commission mistakes, 156
Common knowledge, 20–21
Communication
  channels, 147–148
  Doing What Matters and, 152–159
  eight stages of, 147–149
  execution and, 151–152
  exercises, 160–162
  at GE, 139–140
  guiding coalition for, 147–148

hourglass structure and, 140, 152
importance of, 140, 152
inclusive, 144
interruptions and, 145–146
of key messages, 140–144, 152
linkage in, 143, 148
management style and, 149
memorable leadership and, 150–151
organizational assessment of, 161–162
pitfalls, 148–149
plan-on-a-page for, 143–144, 152, 161
about scope and scale, 19–20
strategies, 147
summarized, 152
SWOT and, 141
in team charter, 120, 133, 136
urgency of, 141, 147–148
vision and, 144–149, 152
Community, in seven Cs, 48, 61
Companies. *See also specific companies*
  brand companies, 27–30
  culture of, 149, 179
  franchises, 71
  lessons learned from, 3, 11–13
  in seven Cs, 48–49, 61
  successes of, 6
Compensation, vision aligned with, 146
Competencies/core skills, 210
Competition. *See also* Strategic
    competitive advantage
  among employees, 156
  implications of, 77
Competitive frame, 202–203
Competitors, in seven Cs, 48–49, 61
Conant, Doug, 145–146
Confidentiality, 156, 158
Connect the dots, 26–31, 33–34, 37.
    See also Linkage
Consensus, 158
Consumer
  in direct-to-consumer model, 29–30
  insights, 203–207
  in seven Cs, 48, 61
Contingency strategies, 108, 114
Convergent thinking, 41, 58, 83
Coppertop battery, 7
Core skills, 210
Core strategy, 114
Cosmetics, 108–112
Costs
  of initiatives, 126–127
  quality and, 154
Crystal Light, 73–74

Culture, changes anchored in, 149, 179
Cupcakes, 11–12
Customer, in seven Cs, 48, 61

Data
  bucket, 41, 61
  convergent thinking and, 41
  reliance on, 20–23, 32, 34, 36–37, 191
Dean Foods, 84–85
Decision making
  consensus in, 158
  data-based, 20–23
  expectations for, 155
  by managers, 157
  quick, 154
  simple approach to, 1–3
  strategies and, 101–114
  teams and, 121–123
Del Monte Company, 175–177
Deliverables, in team charter, 120–121,
    133, 135–136
DeMartini, Rob, 27–30
Deodorant, 69
Developing markets, 67, 86
Development, 169
Direct-to-consumer model, 29–30
Discipline, 157–158
Divergent thinking, 41–42, 83
Doing What Matters (Kilts, Manfredi,
    and Lorber), 152–159
Dorrance, Anson, 163–164
Drawing, 27
Dumb mistakes, 156
Duracell Company, 6–9, 25, 56

Economic climate, 61
80-20 rule, 24
Eliot, T. S., 183
Employees
  competition among, 156
  expectations of, 155
Enablers, 107, 125
Entrepreneurial start-ups, 183–184
Environment, 61
Essential factors, 107
Execution
  accountability for, 128–129, 134, 137
  building blocks of, 151–152
  choices reviewed for, 123–126
  communication and, 151–152
  exercises, 134–138
  failure of, 117–118
  of good ideas, 155

of initiatives, 118–121, 123–138
  organizational assessment of, 138
  road map to success of, 127, 137–138
  SCA and, 119, 123
  situation assessment and, 118
  in small businesses, 129–132
  of strategies, 117–119, 121, 132–135
  summarized, 133–134
  by teams, 118–126, 128–129, 133–138
  umbrella statement and, 118
  vision and, 144
  working backwards in, 127–128
*Execution: The Discipline of Getting
    Things Done* (Bossidy and Charan),
    117–118
Expectations, of employees, 155

Facts
  analysis of, 157
  convergent thinking and, 41
  in organizational alignment survey, 191
  reliance on, 20–23, 32, 34, 36–37, 191
Failure, learning from, 156
Financial element, balanced goals and,
    90–92, 98
Flow, areas of, 177
Frameworks, TTW, 41
  exercises, 60–62
  populating, 62
  seven Cs, 48–49, 52, 58, 61–63
Franchises, 71
Freedom, of managers, 154, 157
Functional advantages, 210

General Electric (GE), 139–140
Generation 2020, 184
Generation X, 184
Generational differences, 184
Gillette
  global anchoring of, 166–167
  Husain at, 175–177
  Kilts at, 146, 149, 152–153, 156–158,
    166–167
  strategies at, 166–167
  strengths and weaknesses of, 153
  TTW and, 6–7, 88, 92, 146, 149, 153,
    156–158, 166–167, 175–176
Global anchoring, 166–167
Goals
  balanced, 90–92, 95, 97–99
  challenging, 94–95
  creating, 98–99
  exercises for, 97–99

Goals *(continued)*
  governing statement and, 90–95
  in hourglass, 41
  organizational assessment of, 99
  SMART, 97–99
  strategies linked to, 107, 110, 112
  summarized, 95–96
  3Ms of, 93–94
  vision and, 90–99
Good ideas, execution of, 155
"Gotchas," 153
Governing statement
  of Braun, 87–88
  exercises, 96–97
  goals and, 90–95
  hourglass structure and, 87
  for individuals, 94–95
  linkage and, 90
  of P&G, 86–87
  as restraining, 87–90
  scope and, 90
  vision and, 83, 85–92, 95
  of WhiteWave, 88
Green Mountain Coffee, 10, 84,
    104–105, 168–169
Guiding coalition, 147–148

Haecker, Kelly, 88
Harvard Innovation Center, 183
Healthcare insurance, 89–90
Hershey Foods, 175
Holbrook, Jim, 165
Horizon Milk, 85, 88
Hourglass structure
  communication and, 140, 152
  convergent thinking in, 41, 58, 83
  divergent thinking in, 41–42, 83
  goals in, 41
  governing statement and, 87
  objectives in, 41
  process of, 40–42, 46–47, 54, 58–59,
      69, 79, 83–84, 87, 95, 101–102,
      140, 144, 152, 183–187
  strategies in, 41–42, 101–102, 112
  turned over, 183–187
  vision in, 83–84, 91, 95, 144
Human resources (HR), 89–90, 174–178
Humor, 158
Husain, Asad, 175–177

Iacocca, Lee, 140
Impact
  degree of, 123–125
  in key message, 140–143, 160

Implications
  defined, 75
  exercises, 80
  of increased competition, 77
  of insights, 41, 79
  key issues and, 75–79
  of low brand awareness, 77
  of regulations, 78
  of store traffic, 78
  summarized, 79
  of technology, 78
Individuals, governing statement for,
    94–95
Information
  flow of, 177
  quality of, 157
In-house capability, 125
Initiatives
  accepting, 131–132
  charter for, 119–121
  choice of, 123–126
  costs of, 126–127
  degree of impact on, 123–125
  execution of, 118–121, 123–138
  identified, 42, 126–127, 134–135
  management of, 126–127, 134
  new ventures, 131
  in plan-on-a-page, 143–144
  rejecting, 131–132
  scope of, 126–127
  small business, 129–132
  strategies and, 118–119, 131–132
  teams and, 118–119
  time of, 126–127
Inner city school, SWOT analysis
    of, 53
Innovation, 155, 187
Insights
  actionable, 74–75
  consumer, 203–207
  exercises, 80–81
  finding, 69–70
  implications of, 41, 79
  of Keurig, 72–73
  key issues and, 71–75, 79
  of Kraft, 73–74
  in marketing, 72
  quality of, 157
  strategies inspired by, 102–105
  summarized, 79
Integrity, 149, 153, 155–156
Interdependencies, in team charter,
    120–121, 133, 136
International Delight, 85

Interruptions, communication and, 145–146

Issues. *See also* Key issues; Vital few
  picture of, 27
  scale of, 19–20
  scope of, 18–20, 32, 34, 36–37
  tough, 155–156
  wall of, 80–81

Jamba Juice
  SCA of, 57–58
  TTW and, 57–58, 68, 70–71
  umbrella statement of, 70
  White at, 68, 70–71
Joe, Father, 185–187
Jokes, 158

Kanter, Rosabeth Moss, 164–165
Kaplan, Sara, 184
K-Cup Pack, 104
Kellogg Executive Leadership Institute
  (KELI), 146
Keurig
  Green Mountain Coffee, 10, 84,
    104–105, 168–169
  insights of, 72–73
  Moran at, 84, 145
  partnerships with, 105–106
  patent expiration and, 104–106
  SCA of, 104, 106–107
  Stacy at, 10, 104–106, 168–169
  strategies of, 104–107
  TTW and, 10, 43, 72–73, 84,
    104–107, 145, 168–169
  umbrella statement of, 43
  vision of, 84, 145
Key issues
  of church, 186
  exercises, 80–81
  implications and, 75–79
  insights and, 71–75, 79
  list of, 41
  of Nutrition Nation, 75–78
  in organizational assessment, 82
  statement of, 68
  summarized, 79
  umbrella statements and, 79
Key messages
  action in, 140–143, 160
  communication of, 140–144, 152
  exercises for, 160–161
  impact in, 140–143, 160
  overview of, 42
  projection of, 147–148

  scope in, 141–142
  situation in, 140–143, 160
  template for, 160
  vital few in, 141
Key performance indicators, 135–136
Kilts, Jim
  Doing What Matters by, 152–159
  at Gillette, 146, 149, 152–153,
    156–158, 166–167
  vision of, 146
Kohinoor Consulting, 129–132
Kotter, John P., 147–149
Kraft, 73–74, 146, 166
Krispy Kreme Doughnuts, 74

Land O'Lakes, 85
Latino market, 109–111, 119–121,
  123–126
Leaders
  change and, 164–165
  memorable, 150–151
  team of, 156
  vision of, 145–147
Leadership Sustainability (Smallwood
  and Ulrich), 165
Leaks, 156
Leckie, Mark, 6–9
Lego, 9–10
Levitt, Theodore, 72
Licensing, 71
Linkage, 26–31, 34, 37, 118
  alignment and, 154
  in communication, 143, 148
  governing statements and, 90
  in organizational alignment survey, 192
Liquidity, 71
Long-term deliverables, 120–121
Long-term potential, 10
Long-term success, 165, 179
Lorber, Robert L., 152–159
Lunchables, 72

Majority rule, 122
Malls, 78
Management
  accountability of, 154
  education, 147
  freedom of, 154, 157
  of initiatives, 126–127, 134
  performance, 171–173, 177
  philosophy, 154–155
  style, 149, 153–154
Mandela, Nelson, 164
Manfredi, John F., 152–159

Marketing. *See also* Situation Assessment Diagnostic
  brand, 28, 154
  insights in, 72
  segments, 110–111
Marketplace, balanced goals and, 90–92, 98
Matrixed organization, 154
Measures, in 3Ms, 93–94, 97–98
Meetings
  accountability and, 171
  casual, 159
  guidelines for, 170–171
  process of, 171
  productive, 169–173, 179
  template for, 170
  weekly, 151, 157–159
Meister, Jeanne, 184
Membership, 119–121, 133, 135
Messages. *See* Key messages
Metrics, in 3Ms, 93–94, 97–98
Mexico, 73–74
Michelangelo, 94
Mickey Mouse, 55
Milestones, in 3Ms, 93–94, 97–98
Millennials, 9, 108–111, 184
Mistakes, 156–157
Moran, Dave, 84, 145
Movie rentals, 11
Must-haves, 107

Natural Balance, 178
Netflix, 11
Network diagram, 136–137
New Balance, 27–31, 103, 125–126
Nike, 28–29
90-10 rule, 24, 75
"No" Trumps "Yes" voting system, 123
Nonprofits, 185–187
Norgaard, Mette, 145–146
Note Storm, 137
Nutrition Nation, 75–78

Objectives
  in hourglass, 41
  in Situation Assessment Diagnostic, 198–200
  strategies tied to, 171
  in team charter, 120, 133, 135
Omission mistakes, 156
One-on-ones, 159
Online channel strategies, 78
Open mind, 16–17
Opinions, 21–23, 37, 191

Opportunities
  of Nutrition Nation, 76
  in SWOT analysis, 50–53, 56–57, 59, 62–63, 76, 198
Oral-B
  Stacy at, 39–40, 46–49, 52–53, 168
  SWOT analysis, 52
  TTW and, 39–40, 46–49, 52–53, 168
  umbrella statement of, 46–47
Organic baby food, 119–121, 123–128
Organization
  balanced goals and, 90–92, 95, 97–99
  capabilities of, 124–125
  matrixed, 154
  readiness of, 124–125
  risk-averse, 156
Organizational alignment survey, 189–195
Organizational assessment
  of anchoring change, 181–182
  of communication, 161–162
  of execution, 138
  of goals, 99
  key issues in, 82
  principles and practices, 37–38, 64–65, 82–83, 99, 114–115, 138, 161–162, 181–182
  process, 64–65
  of strategies, 114–115
  of vision, 99
Oscar Mayer, 72
Outstanding performance, 155

Parents, tough issues and, 155–156
Pareto principle, 24
Partnerships, 105–106
Passive voice, 21
Patent expiration, 104–106
People
  balanced goals and, 90–91, 98
  flow of, 177
Performance
  appraisal, 147
  key indicators, 135–136
  management, 171–173, 177
  outstanding, 155
  TTW enhancing, 184
Personal TTW applications, 185
P&G. *See* Procter & Gamble
Plan B, 108, 114
Planning
  annual, 151–152, 184
  in organizational alignment survey, 194–195

Plan-on-a-page
  alignment and, 144, 152
  exercise, 161
  initiatives in, 143–144
  as living document, 144
  for strategic growth, 143–144
  for TTW, 143–144, 152, 161
Politics, 61
Position, vision and, 83, 87, 90–91, 96
Post Foods, 165
Principles, TTW
  challenge assumptions, 16–18, 32–33,
    35, 37, 189–190
  checklist, 37–38
  as compass, 34
  connect the dots, 26–31, 33–34, 37
  exercises, 35–38
  focus on the vital few, 23–26, 32–34,
    36–37, 75, 111–112
  organizational assessment and, 37–38,
    64–65, 82–83, 99, 114–115, 138,
    161–162, 181–182
  overview of, 15, 33–34
  process and, 40
  rely on facts and data, 20–23, 32, 34,
    36–37, 191
  results of, 31–33
  scope the issue, 18–20, 32, 34, 36–37,
    90, 191–192
Prius, 55
Problem solving, 155
Process
  annual planning, 151–152, 184
  flow, 40–42, 58
  of hourglass structure, 40–42, 46–47,
    54, 58–59, 69, 79, 83–84, 87, 95,
    101–102, 140, 144, 152, 183–187
  meeting, 171
  in organizational alignment survey, 193
  organizational assessment, 64–65
  TTW principles and, 40
Procter & Gamble (P&G)
  governing statement of, 86–87
  Husain at, 175–176
  Shirley at, 67, 69–70, 86–87, 150
  TTW and, 67, 69–70, 86–87, 150, 158,
    167, 175–176
  umbrella statement of, 86
Productive meetings, 169–173, 179
Project Management Institute, 118
Promises, 154
Purpose, vision and, 83, 87, 90–91, 96

Quality, cost and, 154

Quarterly building blocks, 151–152
Quarterly review, 147
Question-and-answer session, 147

Reality, confronting, 153
Recipe, for change, 165
Recognition, 173–174, 179
Recruitment, 164
Regulations, 61, 77–78
Rely on facts and data, 20–23, 32, 34,
    36–37, 191
Results, road map based on, 127, 137–138
Revenue, peaks and valleys of, 130
Rewards, 173–174
Risk-averse organization, 156
Road map to success, 127, 137–138
Ryan, Nolan, 54–55

SCA. *See* Strategic competitive advantage
Scalzo, Joe, 85
Schwartz, Tony, 19
Scope
  communication about, 19–20
  creep, 18
  governing statements and, 90
  of initiatives, 126–127
  of issues, 18–20, 32, 34, 36–37
  in key message, 141–142
  in organizational alignment survey,
    191–192
  principle of, 18–20, 32, 34, 36–37, 90,
    191–192
Second-class citizen syndrome, 34
Seven Cs
  category, 48, 61
  colleagues, 48, 61
  community, 48, 61
  company, 48–49, 61
  competitors, 48–49, 61
  consumer, 48, 61
  customer, 48, 61
  as TTW framework, 48–49, 52, 58,
    61–63
Sharing, 155
Shirley, Ed, 67, 69–70, 86–87, 150
Short-term deliverables, 120–121
Short-term wins, 149
Show of thumbs, 122–123
Signals, 165, 179
Significance/objectives, in team charter,
    120, 133, 135
Silk soy milk, 85, 88
Silos, leveling, 155
Simply Effective (Ashkenas), 184

Situation
    assessment, 48, 73, 118, 150, 186,
        198–210
    in key message, 140–143, 160
Situation Assessment Diagnostic
    business objectives/current state of the
        business, 198–200
    category dynamics, 200–201
    competencies/core skills, 210
    competitive frame, 202–203
    consumer insights, 203–207
    overview of, 198
    value proposition and delivery,
        208–209
Skin care, 108–112
Sloppy writing, 19
Small business initiatives, 129–132
Smallwood, Norm, 165
SMART goals, 97–99
Smart mistakes, 156–157
Smartphones, 12
Soccer, 163–164
Social trends, 61
South Africa, 164
Specialty retailers, 29–31
Stacy, Michelle
    at Keurig, 10, 104–106, 168–169
    at Oral-B, 39–40, 46–49, 52–53, 168
Stakeholders, 128–129, 138, 159
STEEP, 61
Store traffic, 78
Strategic competitive advantage (SCA)
    execution and, 119, 123
    of Jamba Juice, 57–58
    of Keurig, 104, 106–107
    strategies leveraging, 102, 107, 113, 123
    SWOT analysis and, 54–57, 64
    vision and, 84, 95
Strategies
    actions for, 117–119, 121, 132–133
    aha moments inspiring, 102–104
    alternative, 114
    annual planning process, 151–152, 184
    best choice of, 107–112
    of BetterFace, 108–112
    brainstorming, 102–103
    communication, 147
    contingency, 108, 114
    core, 114
    decision making and, 101–114
    degree of impact on, 123–125
    execution of, 117–119, 121, 132–135
    exercises for, 113–115, 134–135

    at Gillette, 166–167
    goals linked to, 107, 110, 112
    growth, plan-on-a-page for, 143–144
    in hourglass structure, 41–42,
        101–102, 112
    identifying, 113–114
    initiatives and, 118–119, 131–132
    insights inspiring, 102–105
    of Keurig, 104–107
    levels of, 114
    objectives tied to, 171
    organizational assessment of,
        114–115
    SCA and, 102, 107, 113, 123
    simple approach to, 1–3
    summarized, 112–113
    SWOT analysis and, 102, 108–111, 113
    think-plan-act in, 2, 6
    vital few in, 111–112
Strengths
    of Gillette, 153
    of Nutrition Nation, 76
    in SWOT analysis, 49–53, 55–57,
        62–63, 76, 198
Success
    of companies, 6
    as habit forming, 13
    long-term, 165, 179
    road map to, 127, 137–138
    vision for, 83–86, 90, 93, 95
Superlatives, 21
SWOT analysis
    of All Clean, 55–57
    of BetterFace, 108–111
    of church, 185–186
    communication and, 141
    done right, 53–54
    exercises, 62–64
    of inner city school, 53
    matrix, 50–51, 62–63
    of Nutrition Nation, 75–76
    opportunities in, 50–53, 56–57, 59,
        62–63, 76, 198
    of Oral-B, 52
    SCA and, 54–57, 64
    strategies and, 102, 108–111, 113
    strengths in, 49–53, 55–57, 62–63,
        76, 198
    threats in, 50–53, 56, 58–59,
        62–63, 198
    vision and, 84, 95
    weaknesses in, 49–53, 55–56,
        62–63, 198

Symbols, 165, 179

Teachers, tough issues and, 155–156
Team charter
    assumptions, 120–121, 133
    deliverables, 120–121, 133, 135–136
    for execution, 119–121, 135–136
    exercises, 135–137
    interdependencies, 120–121, 133, 136
    membership, 119–121, 133, 135
    network diagram, 136–137
    significance/objectives, 120, 133, 135
    timing/communication, 120, 133, 136
Teams
    choices reviewed by, 123–126
    creation of, 119–121
    decision making and, 121–123
    execution by, 118–126, 128–129,
        133–138
    initiatives and, 118–119
    of leaders, 156
    summarized, 133–134
    voting by, 122–123
Technology, 61, 78
Think to Win (TTW). *See also* Change,
        anchoring of; Communication;
        Execution; Frameworks, TTW;
        Hourglass structure; Principles,
        TTW; Situation Assessment
        Diagnostic; Strategies; Vision
    All Clean and, 55–57
    benefits of, 5–6, 12–13
    BetterFace and, 108–112
    Braun and, 87–88
    Del Monte and, 175–177
    Duracell and, 6–9, 25, 56
    end of, as beginning, 179, 183–187
    exercises, 35–38, 59–65, 80–82, 96–99,
        113–115, 134–138, 160–162,
        179–182
    future relevance of, 183–184
    at GE, 139–140
    Gillette and, 6–7, 88, 92, 146, 149, 153,
        156–158, 166–167, 175–176
    introduction to, 1–3
    Jamba Juice and, 57–58, 68, 70–71
    Keurig and, 10, 43, 72–73, 84,
        104–107, 145, 168–169
    key to, 67–79
    Lego and, 9–10
    as mindset, 15
    New Balance and, 27–31, 103, 125–126
    new thinking in, 5–13
    for nonprofits, 185–187

Oral-B and, 39–40, 46–49, 52–53, 168
    performance enhanced by, 184
    personal applications of, 185
    P&G and, 67, 69–70, 86–87, 150, 158,
        167, 175–176
    plan-on-a-page for, 143–144, 152, 161
    Post Foods and, 165
    power of, 2
    process flow, 40–42, 58
    umbrella statements in, 41–47, 50, 58,
        60, 62
    WhiteWave Foods and, 84–85,
        88–89, 103
Think-plan-act, 2, 6
Threats
    of Nutrition Nation, 76
    in SWOT analysis, 50–53, 56, 58–59,
        62–63, 198
3Ms, 93–94, 96–98
THRIVE baby food, 119–121, 123–128
Thumbs, show of, 122–123
Time, of initiatives, 126–127
Timeliness, 40
Timing/communication, in team charter,
    120, 133, 136
"Tired of Strategic Planning"
    (Beinhocker and Kaplan), 184
Top-down dictums, 153, 155
Total Brand Value, 154
Touch-Points (Conant and Norgaard),
    145–146
Tough issues, 155–156
Toyota, 55
Traditionalists, 184
Training, 169
TTW. *See* Think to Win
Tunnel vision, 26
The 2020 Workplace (Meister and
    Willyerd), 184

UConn women's basketball team,
    163–164
Ulrich, Dave, 165
Ultra battery, 7–8, 25
Umbrella statements
    alignment on, 43–44, 68, 70
    defined, 41, 44, 58
    execution and, 118
    exercise, 60
    ineffective, 45
    of Jamba Juice, 70
    of Keurig, 43
    key issues and, 79
    of Oral-B, 46–47

Umbrella statements *(continued)*
 of P&G, 86
 strong, 44–45
 in TTW, 41–47, 50, 58, 60, 62
University of North Carolina women's
  soccer, 163–164
Urgency, 141, 147–148
Value proposition and delivery, 208–209
Victory, declared too soon, 149
Vision
 actionable, 84, 95
 aliveness of, 144–146
 of BetterFace, 110
 characteristics of, 84, 95
 communication and, 144–149, 152
 compensation aligned with, 146
 execution and, 144
 exercises, 96–99
 of GE, 140
 goals and, 90–99
 governing statement and, 83, 85–92, 95
 in hourglass structure, 83–84, 91,
   95, 144
 of Keurig, 84, 145
 of Kilts, 146
 lack of, 148
 of leaders, 145–147
 obstacles to, 148–149
 organizational assessment of, 99
 projection of, 147
 purpose and position in, 83, 87,
   90–91, 96
 realizable, 84, 95
 SCA and, 84, 95
 statement, 83

 for success, 83–86, 90, 93, 95
 summarized, 95–96
 SWOT and, 84, 95
 tunnel, 26
 of WhiteWave Foods, 84–85
Vital few
 focus on, 23–26, 32–34, 36–37, 75,
   111–112
 in key messages, 141
 maximum number of, 75
 in organizational alignment survey, 190
 in strategies, 111–112
Voting, 122–123

Wall, writing on, 19
Weaknesses
 of Gillette, 153
 of Nutrition Nation, 76
 in SWOT analysis, 49–53, 55–56,
   62–63, 198
Weekly building blocks, 151–152
Weekly meetings, 151, 157–159
Welch, Jack, 139–140, 145–146
West, Dave, 175, 177
White, James D., 68, 70–71
WhiteWave Foods, 84–85, 88–89, 103
"Why Good Strategies Fail: Lessons for
  the C-Suite" (Project Management
  Institute), 118
Widget illustration, 141–142
Willyerd, Karie, 184
Winning (Welch), 145
Work, flow of, 177
Working backwards, 127–128
Writing, 19